CHECKLIST
FOR
PUBLISHING & SELLING YOUR BOOKS

By
Rex Lee Reynolds

First North American Serial Rights
Foreign Language Rights
Foreign English Language Rights
Audio & Electronic Rights

CHECKLIST
FOR
PUBLISHING & SELLING YOUR BOOKS

Copyright 2010 Rex Lee Reynolds

ISBN: 978-0-557-30781-4

Table Of Contents

Dedication

This book is dedicated to Kent Davis, my good friend for many years and a fellow author, who has always encouraged me in my writing over the years, and is also appreciated for introducing me to a very good publisher.

Forward

A Checklist for Publishing & Selling Your Books came about largely from my wanting to have a something of this kind available for myself for reference, and something to share with a few friends. When getting into writing it down it turned out to be enough to put into a book, and something that in the process brought into mind the idea of checklists for a number of other subjects that will be published as separate checklist books in the future.

Not too many years ago, before the coming of the Internet there was still a lot of information available. You could and still can get a book from the bookstores entitled Writers Market that listed scores of publishing companies, literary agents and others with information about how to contact them, and descriptions of the kind of writers and material they are looking to find and publish.

Many of the ideas, methods and information that can help us become successful might appear to be secret or hidden from us even though they are actually available right at our fingertips, yet at most times not right in front of our eyes. The main idea is to put some of the best information and ideas we can use in a convenient spot, so we can more easily get the best use from them.

When mentioning to friends a couple books of mine that were published in the summer of 2009 a few of the friends replied that they also plan to write a book, which will be their first. Although the information in this can be used by just about anybody, this has been written especially for those who are new to writing and publishing and are looking forward to publishing and selling their first book or books. Having been a writer for many years with experience in success and failure, having done well and making mistakes in the process, it seemed a good idea to put into writing things that others can learn and profit from by having such information easily available.

The primary focus is on the publishing and marketing of your books, tried and proven methods of getting your book or books into the hands of the readers, or methods of increasing your book sales, rather than how to write your books, how to improve the quality of your books, writing methods or author practices and techniques. But at least some of the latter has also been included because it is important to have a very good book if you are going to be able to publish and particularly sell it.

It is sometimes a misconception on the part of new authors that once their book is in print, published and available for sale, that readers will of course buy the book or books. Authors are often sufficiently engrossed in the writing of that wonderful novel or fabulous non-fiction piece, that it is all so easy for them to overlook the simple fact that if no one knows the book is there, no one is going to buy it.

The preceding may seem too simple to be true, but I have seen it many times, myself included when I have created something and naturally assumed everyone else is going to absolutely fall in love with my work, when the fact is that everyone else is not the slightest bit aware that my masterpiece even exists. We will be discussing methods of helping the readers find out about our masterpieces we have created and how they are so very valuable.

Disclaimer

The author, publisher and distributors of this book will in no manner whatsoever assume any responsibility, or liability of any kind for advice or methods provided in this book and used by the reader of this book. The reader assumes all responsibility and liability for his or her actions, as a result of reading this book and using ideas found herein.

In a number of places advice and/or recommendations are given regarding particular companies and their services, and I would like to state that I am in no way employed by any of the companies or services being recommended or suggested, or being paid any fees of any kind for mentioning these companies and their services.

No warrantees or guarantees of any kind are being made or implied by the author or publisher as to the reliability or soundness of any of these companies or services being mentioned or recommended. No liability of any kind whatsoever is or will be assumed by the author or publisher.

CHAPTER ONE

The Basics

The primary purpose of this book is to reveal methods of publishing and selling your books. Many of the things having to do with the writing of your book are covered elsewhere, such as how to write a good story, developing fiction characters and things of that nature. There are many writing schools and other books that can help you a great deal with those subjects. But here we will at least touch upon the basics if only as a reminder, since the basics are essential because without good formatting, correct copyrighting and attention to legal matters, it may not be possible to accomplish the first step of getting your book published, which in turn would mean no one will be buying it.

If you are a very experienced author much of the basics you will already know. There is a Publishing and Selling Checklist at the end of Chapter Two that you can go to at any time that will hopefully give you some new ideas to use. If you are not experienced everything else along with the checklist can be a great deal of help to you.

Index & Table of Contents Tools

Interestingly enough there are still people around who write books on a typewriter. Some people do not use computers. There are also people around who write books with a pencil and are very successful. We all have our own way of doing things. If you do use a computer and your book is going to have a table of contents or an index there is nothing at all wrong with doing them manually, other than the fact that it's way too much work, especially if your book is at all a large book. If you use a computer there is a much better way to go. Even if your book is small the table of contents and index tools can save you a lot of time and work. An automated table of contents is a very nice convenience when editing your book since it can be hyper-linked to the sections of your book it describes.

If you are writing your book with some kind of word processing software such as Microsoft Word, and if you are writing a non-fiction book you will undoubtedly want to include a table of contents and maybe an index. With MS Word you can save yourself a lot of time and work by using the table of contents feature by selecting different sized headings and inserting an automated table of contents at the beginning of your book. The same thing can be done with an index tool by marking the words or phrases you want in the index, then inserting the index at the end of your book.

When using the automated table of contents it will list the page numbers to the right of your subject if you select that feature, and when editing your book if you click on the page numbers in the table of contents you will be taken to each subject listed. The table of contents can be updated as often as needed while making changes in your book. To learn how to use the automated table of contents and index features, look them up in the Help section of your word processing program. It will only take a few minutes to learn how to use these tools but will be well worth the time spent.

Starting Somewhere

For people who may be very new or even completely new to the subject of writing, it's entirely possible that you might find yourself with an idea for a good story or non-fiction book of some kind, you may have mentioned it to a few friends who encourage you, but the fact remains that you are a little timid about it or just lack the experience, and have managed to put very little of your idea, or maybe not even a single word of it on paper or into your computer.

Many years ago before I had ever even thought of writing a book, I was telling a friend about a story, that happened to be a true story. The friend was an author of a number of fiction books, and I asked my friend if he thought my story would make a good book. His answer to me was some very good advice and something worth passing on. My friend explained to me that the most important thing would be to get the story down on paper. He also mentioned that I shouldn't worry about the first draft and how bad it might seem to me. I could always make improvements to it.

It seems that his advice was and is very good because the fact is that no matter how good the story it actually does not exist anywhere if it's only in somebody's mind. No one else knows about it, and no one is going to know about it until it gets recorded somewhere besides your memory. If you haven't written it down yet, just start writing, no matter how silly or foolish it may seem to you or others with whom you share it. If you don't have it written there is no way in the world you can edit it, change and improve it. Even if you have the memory of an elephant, if it isn't in writing it doesn't exist. And as good a mind as you may have, and as ridiculous as it may sound, it's much harder to edit your story or make improvements to it while it's in your head.

Keeping Notes

And while working on your book it's a good work habit to develop to keep a pencil and some paper handy wherever you are, to write down notes or ideas as you get them, so you don't forget them and neglect to get them in your book. A memo recorder on a cell phones or a good dictation device of some kind works very well for this purpose. I have a very good memory but often find ideas coming to me when I'm sleeping at night, and if I'm fortunate enough to remember them when I wake up, I keep a recording device of some kind next to my bed to record notes. If I wake up in the middle of the night with an idea I record it immediately for later use, if not get up and work on the writing of the idea while it's still fresh in my mind.

Grammar

Most of us know or should know if our grammar and spelling is up to par. If we don't know or are not quite sure about it we should ask someone to review some of our writing and get an opinion, or compare our writing to the writing of others that we are certain are using good grammar. If it happens that you are certain that book composition and/or grammar are not really your thing you can still write a book. There are two ways to go. You can either learn, which can be a matter of a lot of practice and can take a long time, or you can get someone to help you with those things, in addition to your word-processor that can also help you with the grammar. If fact, if you prefer you can hire someone to do it all for you, write the book, edit it, publish and market it. There are people around who will do it all for you if you just give them your ideas and pay them to do it.

If you are not quite sure about your grammar and you want to get your book written and published in the not too distant future it would be advisable to get some help. If you do not have a friend with the grammar skills to help you as a favor, or who is willing to do a work for hire for you or co-author with you, there are many services available for hire that can help you get your book into acceptable reading format. These services can be found by searching the Internet for subjects such as "Using Good Grammar, How To Publish A Book" etc. There are also a lot of good dictionaries and thesauruses online than can be of great assistance to you in the writing and composition of your book if you choose to go the route of learning rather than hiring someone.

Reader Education Level

Although some of us may not agree, an important thing to keep in mind when writing your book is keeping it in as simple to read as possible. Some people make the mistake of using a lot of big words that many readers would stumble on. If you happen to be a very educated college PHD kind of person, keep in mind when writing your book that many or possibly most the people reading your book may not have quite the high level of education and vocabulary that you do. In fact, it may come as a surprise to some that there is a terrible illiteracy problem that has existed for a long time in this country, which you need to account for when writing your book by making it as easy to read as possible for all who read it. You will find that many of the people who can read and write will have problems understanding what you are writing if you

14

use a college level vocabulary. If you happen to be writing a book targeted specifically toward highly educated people, then that is fine. But otherwise it's best to use a grade school or high school vocabulary at most in order to make your work understandable to all your readers.

Submission Format

When submitting a manuscript to an agent or publisher be sure to remember to use the submission guidelines provided by the agent or publisher. An inexperienced writer that produces an exceptionally good book in its content can probably get away with just about any kind of format, but will have much better chances of success by following standard format guidelines when submitting a manuscript to any kind of publisher, conventional or otherwise. If a manuscript is submitted with sloppy grammar, a lot of typos, incorrect line spacing and margins, a conventional publisher may be willing to work with it if the publisher feels there is a good enough story or good enough content that really is of interest, but don't count on it, particularly if the publisher does not feel that your manuscript will not be something good enough to be on a best seller list. At best, if a publisher completely loves your work but can see that your grammar and format need some work, maybe he or she will suggest someone you can contact to help you with those problems.

When writing your manuscript follow the guidelines suggested by your publisher, which will probably be the essential things such as using the same font throughout the entire manuscript, double-line spacing and one-inch margins on each side, with headers and footers showing the book's title and your name at the top and page numbers at the bottom.

Submission Templates

If you plan to do what is referred to as self-publishing and are going to submit your manuscript to a POD (print on demand) publisher that publisher will likely have templates available for your use at no charge that will be a big help to you in formatting your book. An example of such a POD publisher is the publisher of this book, LuLu Publishing at www.lulu.com, which has many such templates available. There are other POD publishers available as well with a good many useful publishing tools.

Templates available for the various sizes of books such as paperback, hardcover, 6x9 etc., are in word processing format with the margins, line spacing, page numbering etc. preset into the template. This makes it easy to insert your manuscript into the template so the formatting of your book will come out like you want. You can use a template exactly as is or make modifications if you prefer.

After hearing about LuLu Publishing from a friend I was sufficiently impressed with the company and their website that I selected it as a publisher without even doing any research on other POD publishers. I had two books sitting around for a year or two and unpublished because all I got back from agents and publishers was rejection slips, after having sent many query letters. The same two books that had been collecting dust got published with LuLu in just a matter of a few weeks at almost no cost to me. In fact there had been dozens of query letters to agents and publishers with results amounting to only a "thank you but not interested" reply from all of them.

I like LuLu's online tutorials and tools that make publishing a book so easy and cost effective. The actual cost to me for getting both books published, into print and available for download was less than $20 per book. Compare that with the hundreds or thousands of dollars that other publishers want to publish a book and you will see that it's an impressive difference.

After publishing my two books with LuLu, seeing the books on Google Book Search and Amazon, I started to write this book and did some research on the POD publishers and found that I had made a good choice by going with LuLu. They use a very attractive 80/20 revenue sharing system with the authors, have a very comprehensive and useful website, no charge to join, no setup fees, and have many attractive distribution plans available. LuLu acquired weRead, which automatically lists your books that are published with LuLu and allows authors to interface their books and suggest them to your friends that are FaceBook users.

But don't take my word for it, or anyone else's either. You should always do your homework and be sure to research and confirm information to make sure you are on the right track. Then make your own decision based upon the data you collected from your research. In the process of making decisions about which publisher to go with, many people will of course research the subject of publishers very well before selecting one, and they should. There is a great deal of information available online about publishers and how to chose one, as well as books available that are dedicated entirely to the subject.

The publisher's major role is helping you get your book into print. A publisher also can be very helpful in assisting you to market and sell books, but the marketing and sales of your book is only one of many things the publisher deals with, and it can be of utmost importance to you to not take for granted that the publisher is going to do everything, and pay as much attention as possible to the sales process in order to maximize sales.

When submitting your completed work to the publisher, whether by uploading it online or through the regular mail on paper, it is vital to have your book formatted correctly, so the publisher will be able to finalize it and put it into print. For example the margins must be correct. If you submit a manuscript to a publisher, editor or agent with margins that are too narrow, the editor, agent or publisher may have an awkward time even reading your work, let alone putting it into print.

While browsing in a bookstore and looking through a paperback I was shocked to find a typo on one of the pages. I had never seen such a thing in all my years in school or after, and just kept looking at it and other people in the bookstore, wondering if they knew about it, and asked myself how it could have possibly happened. It probably doesn't happen often but it's possible and does happen. The standards are very high. That was the first one I saw and have not seen many since in printed books, except books of my own sent to me by a publisher which embarrassing and taught me to be more careful.

Corrections and Rewrites

The process of proofing our final copy before submitting for publishing is very important. The late and great Isaac Asimov, Russian American, most known for his science fiction writing, said some years before passing away that he was finally able to do it right the first time, meaning that he completed a book when writing it the first time, without re-writing or editing it. I never really got that good, and I do recall going through books many times after the first writing in order to catch my typos and other errors.

In the good old days before the use of computers with spellcheckers or before the Internet was even dreamed of the best of authors were maybe be so good they never made a typo. On the otherhand and possibly closer to the truth, maybe this guy with a number of bestsellers under his belt could dash off a book loaded with typos and garbage all through it, that would have to be corrected by the agent's or editor's forlorn and frustrated secretary, who would really like to get the address of the author so she could find him, and vent her frustrations by torturing him for a very long time.

Likewise the grammer is very important, and fortunately these days the wordprocessors are often a great deal of help to us with the grammar as well, but they will not do everything for us. Many years ago, not being very successful at much of anything, and decided to do at least one thing for myself, if I didn't manage to accomplish anything else, which was to learn how to write, or at least improve my skills in written communication the best I could. And looking at the writing of a good many of my friends, this would be some good advice for them as well. It doesn't mean that people are stupid by any means, it just means they could use a little practice, or maybe even a lot of practice.

If you are like Asimov and are able to do it right the first time then you will not need this. But a tool that has been most helpful to me in proofing a book is an electronic text-to-speech reader, which reads the text when copied to the clipboard of your computer. I have written several books using this tool and found it very helpful in catching errors that I could hear, and that I somehow missed with my eyes. There are a number of the readers around and for free or with a free trial and don't cost much if anything. The one being used to help proof this book is called Speakonia which may be obtained for free at http://www.cfs-technologies.com/home/.

No electronic device will ever be able to completely replace the vast and intricate capabilities of the human eye or mind. If you use the text-to-speech reader you will still have to use your eyes. But I cannot emphasise enough how valuable one of these text-to-speech readers can be as an aid in proofing your book. I find it most valuable when proofing a book and find many times where I meant to use the word your and had typed the word you. The word reader will help you notice your typo when you hear it. For example, you wanted to use the word "clever" but instead you mistakenly typed the word "cleaver." When you hear the word "cleaver" being spoken by your text-to-speech device, it will sound like something you use to chop meat with, rather than something in reference to a smart person. On the otherhand for words that have different spellings and meanings but sound the same, such as there and their, the book reader will not help you with this, and you will have to rely on your eyes.

Other valuable tools are the dictionary and thesaurus for finding the correct meaning of words. The spellchecker and thesaurus in your wordprocessor can be of help, and there are many dictionaries online that can easily be used to determine the correct definition of a word or words, and will show all definitions for the same words. Two words that sound the same such as steel and steal can easily be looked up with an online dictionary or thesaurus, in order for you to use the correct word in your sentences.

Copyrights

Your book is automatically copyrighted when it is published, when it's first put into print, but a copyright and a registered copyright are two different things. You would most likely be fine and never have a problem by simply getting your book published, at which point you would legally own the copyright to your book. But it does not hurt anything at all and is in fact a good idea to register the copyright of your book with the Library of Congress, just to be safe in the event that someone else ever wanted to make claim to the rights to your book. The cost is about $35 per book, and you can print out the form from the Library of Congress at http://www.copyright.gov/ or file for your copyright registration online at the Library of Congress website. The website has a lot of very informative material about copyright law that you may find useful.

CHAPTER TWO

What To Write

You're all dressed up and deciding where you want to go. If it happens that you haven't written your book yet and are deciding exactly what it is you are going to write, you may want to keep in mind that non-fiction can be easier to sell than fiction. And many of us would tend to tell you as well that non-fiction might be easier to write, particularly if it's your first book, since fiction may likely require skills that may take longer to develop than non-fiction. Either way, many good writers of both fiction and non-fiction may write quite a number of books before ever getting one published. Sometimes it's all about getting the experience.

Fiction can also at times be considered more of a luxury for readers, something they may enjoy in their leisure, and although they may get ideas for fiction books for things that could help them, it's more likely they will get more benefit from a non-fiction book, in the way of things they can apply to their work life, personal life etc. Particularly in difficult financial times many people would be more likely to buy a book about how to improve their career before they would buy a fiction mystery novel. And if you do decide on a non-fiction book to start, and it looks like it will be quite a large book, if possible you may want to consider cutting it up and writing a number or series of smaller books encompassing all the material of the one large book. We see this with fiction and non-fiction as well. The books for Dummies non-fiction group and the Harry Potter fiction books for example. See Bundle Marketing, Chapter 5, page 51.

If you have not yet decided what your book is going to be about keep the following in mind when making your decision. Realize very well that to sell your book there is a not so little thing called supply and demand, which makes the entire world run. You need to create a book that everybody wants, that everybody is looking for, and that hopefully only you have. That will be a winning combination that will put you over the top, even if you go to a remote island somewhere with no communication with the outside world. If your book is in big demand your readers will find you and get that book from you. If your book is only mediocre or worse, you of course can still sell it, but you will have the very awkward task of selling ice to people who live at the North Pole, and that can be but may not be at all fun.

Whether you are going to write fiction or non-fiction it's good to keep in mind that many authors do very well with the series of books. If the first book is a seller it makes sense to do a second and maybe a third since people now like your work and may likely buy more of your books on the same or similar subject. A series of cookbooks by a well-known author would likely not find a reader owning only one of the series if the reader really liked the first book. The reader would most likely be inclined to get the other cookbooks by the same author as well. Even if the subjects are different in a series of books, if they like your first book the second can sell better.

If you have already written a book it is up to you to decide if the marketing of your book is doing well or has violated the supply and demand law. None of us want to think about this but in case you didn't know, it is entirely possible to write a book that no one is ever, ever going to buy. Yes, it can and does happen. If you have applied every thing you have learned in this book and maybe a few other sources, and your book is still not selling you may have a bum book on your hands. This is for you to decide and if you decide that you do in fact have a bum book, don't feel too bad, because many of us have been there. Many successful authors can tell you that they wrote a dozen or so books, and maybe even published a few before they got their first sale! So if you decide that you do have a bum book, don't despair too much, just get started writing the next better book that will sell!

So now you have decided what you are going to write or what your next book will be about, or have now completed that wonderful book and need to know exactly what to do with it, maybe have some good ideas, or maybe you don't have the slightest clue.

In what we could call the good old days of writing, the days of yesteryear, as in the 1940ies for example, if you were one of a few good writers that were around you would tap out your book on one of those old typewriters and dash it off to your editor or publisher friend, who doesn't complain at all about your typos and bad grammar, because your name is Hemmingway or you're one of the handful of other good writers of that era, and you are good buddies with the publisher, address him by his first name, have met his family, and just about anything you write will be heavily drooled upon and eaten up with a fork.

And your publisher buddy dashes a letter off back to you, and enthusiastically tells you how he can't wait to put your new book into print, and ends the letter by telling you to give his love to your wife, kids and dog. If that is how life works for you, you certainly live a charmed life and are much envied by many of us. But as we said, those were the good old days, and for most of us who do not live that kind of charmed life, but do have those kinds of daydreams and think that things still work that way now would probably do well to become a little more realistic.

The forgoing is something of an exaggeration, but I actually know writers who do or have been thinking that way. They have read books written by the old guys, learned how it was done, become fans, want to follow in their footsteps and tend to think in terms of methods that went out many decades ago. And the answer to them is the same, get realistic and come into the twenty-first century and start doing things a lot differently. Otherwise we can probably plan on our work that is collecting dust to continue to collect dust until the end of time.

Work Habits

Any successful author can tell us that work habits are of prime importance. We need to make a habit of writing a lot, at least a few thousand words per day to keep the production and continuity going. Make a plan and follow the plan. A little here and a little there, changing horses in the middle of the stream or not staying consistently on the same course of action will get you nowhere quickly.

The work environment also plays a big part in our productivity. If we work at home we have to do a good job of managing the other things in our home lives, so we will be able to get as much as possible of our writing work done. A good quiet workspace in the home is good, where there will be a minimum of interruptions. Sometimes it's nice to get away for a bit, enjoy a change of scenery and get some much-needed exercise between our writing sessions.

With most of us enjoying the convenience of laptop and notebook computers, a coffee shop with the complimentary wireless access can be very nice, if there isn't too many distractions such as music that is playing that is in discord with what we are writing about, or people talking so loud that we cannot concentrate on our work. Staying at the book continually can be a disadvantage and could be what causes what people refer to a writer's block. It's important to get away from it at times, which refreshes out minds when we get back to it. If you think about it you may recall working on something, any kind of project, you get tired of it, take a break, get away from the project and do better when you get back to it. Sometimes when away from it is when the best inspiration is found.

Trying to write a book during the lunch hour at our job can be a little rough. There's nothing wrong with writing a book while we at the same time have a job, but in most cases the two activities will need to be separate. It doesn't set well with most employers when they discover that a good amount of an employee's work time is being devoted to the writing of the employee's book. And with all the electronic devices employers have at their disposal, it is easier than ever for them to see what an employee is doing with the time they spend at the job. Better to spend as much time after work and on the weekends writing the book rather than taking a chance on losing that valuable job.

Setting Goals

Along with establishing the habit of writing a few thousand words per day to keep it going at a good pace, it's good to also establish the habit of setting realistic goals. It will be found that we get more accomplished when we set goals. If you set a goal of having your book completed in sixty days you may not reach your goal. Maybe the goal of sixty days was not realistic; maybe ninety days would have been more realistic. But it is certain that having set a goal of any kind you will accomplish more than if you had not. This has been proven in many kinds of activities and just simply works.

Keep Backup Copies

As much as this may sound unnecessary to mention, to publish and sell a book it has to be somewhere, it has to exist and reside somewhere in order to publish and sell it. The electronic devices we use to create the book and keep it somewhere are nothing short of marvelous. What would we do without them? They just work for us day in and day out and help us get so much work done. But as we know they are not infallible and do at times let us down.

You may have never had the experience and hopefully you never will, but the feeling that comes over you when you have your unpublished manuscript of several hundred pages on the computer hard drive that just quit is something like the most hideous of all feelings. It's a terribly sick feeling in your stomach that comes over you, knowing that so many months of your work is now gone forever, except what you will be able to piece back together from your memory.

It will never happen to me, you say, but it does. Doesn't everybody know they should keep a backup copy of their work? Well, if they do know there are certainly some of us including myself that at one time or another forgot, wasn't paying attention or somehow neglected to make that backup copy and ended up paying dearly for the neglect.

In your word-processing program there is a setting you can select that will automatically make a backup copy of your document every five, ten minutes or in whatever increment you select. Of course if you make your backup copy on the same hard drive that your original document is on, and you hard drive fails this isn't going to do you much good.

The backup copy on the same hard drive can come in handy if the original document gets corrupted, in which case you can use the backup to recover most or hopefully all of your data. But you should keep another backup copy in a location other than the same hard drive as the original document. This can be an external hard drive, removable disc or memory device. If you don't keep an external backup copy your work is at great risk.

Offsite Backup

It's even suggestible to also keep an offsite backup. If you keep your manuscript on the hard drive of your computer at home, and an external backup copy also at home you are very well protected, unless you come home one day and see that your house has somehow burned to the ground. Most of the better I.T. departments of companies have a person from an offsite storage company stop by each day and pick up a box of backup tapes from the I.T. department. All the company's information is on those tapes. The person from the offsite storage company takes the box to a remote location for storage. If something disastrous happens at a company's I.T. department and all the company's data is lost, the offsite storage company will show up with tapes that have a backup of all the company's data.

As authors we don't need to employ an offsite storage company but if we do our writing at home we can apply the same principal by making a copy each day and taking it to the office with us or another location for safekeeping. A more convenient offsite backup method is to transfer a copy each day onto a remote server. It only takes a minute or so to do it. This can be your own web server or someone else's. Many online companies offer storage space on their servers for customers. But if you put a backup of your manuscript on a remote server **make certain you encrypt your manuscript document with a password** before doing so, and keep the password in a safe place where only you will be able to retrieve it. Be sure to remove the encryption from your manuscript document prior to your final uploading it to a publisher for publication.

Legal Matters

If you happen to be looking around for a literary agent you will probably notice that many of them are also attorneys. These are pretty good guys to have around because the legal things are important. You do not in any way have to have an attorney in order to write, publish and sell a book, but if your book deals with particular non-fiction subject matters, or in some cases fiction ideas as well, knowing a good attorney could soon turn him or her into your best friend. With fiction books you will always notice a disclaimer that mentions that none of the characters described in the book are taken from the lives of real people, and any resemblance to real people is purely coincidental.

For example, if you thought it might be a good idea to put a picture of your favorite cartoon character on the cover or inside your book, because you just love that character and it just looks so cute, you would quickly find yourself in a heap of trouble with the registered owner of that cartoon character, the results of which would likely make you feel that you have just arrived at a prison in Guantanamo Bay Detention Camp, along with a bunch of other people also known as terrorists.

More realistically your literary agent, attorney or publisher would be quick to point out to you that you are in violation of copyright or trademark laws, and ask you to remove the cute little mouse from your book, or at least draw a cute little mouse of your own that didn't look like the other guy's mouse. But with today's reliance on electronic contrivances it would be a good idea for you to pay very close attention to these types of things, and in no way rely on your publisher or attorney to catch things like this for you. If all of you missed it you might find yourself in a bad legal situation.

Although much of the legal world can seem quite complicated to many of us, most the legal matters boil down to simple everyday common sense, a lot of which deals with the idea of not stealing other people's stuff. If you wanted to take a number of screen shots from someone's website and use them in your book, you could do this but only with written permission of the owner or manager of the website. And the same with any other materials you put in your book, photos, images, trademarks etc. It's best to create the content yourself and even then make sure it doesn't even resemble something that belongs to someone else. We all need to protect our rights to intellectual properties otherwise everybody and their dogs would be stealing those rights.

Be cautious about publishers that are not in the same country as you, particularly if it appears they are not in the mainstream of things, not well known, cannot b vouched for by someone you know well and don't have the best of reputations. As good as they may look they can easily get out of paying you simply because you would need to go to the country where they are located to collect or contact a lawyer there to do that for you.

If it's the case that you don't feel you need an attorney, and particularly if you do not have a lot of experience in the business world, it is a good idea when doing business of any kind to put things in writing, or a contract between you and the other person or persons with whom you are doing business, with the contract being singed and dated by both and witnessed by a third party. The attorneys would maybe tell us that a verbal agreement, the old handshake agreement sort of thing is a legally binding contract, but we can probably expect the attorneys to also tell us that having a written contract between the two parties carries a lot more weight in the event that a dispute of any kind occurs between the two parties.

It can be to some people's detriment that they tend to shy away from written contracts of any kind. But if they give it a little thought and attention they could easily see that contracts can protect them a great deal. Their reluctance is due to the fact that they do not understand what the contract means, don't have an attorney to explain it to them or don't want to take the time to read and understand the contract, and it would be to their best advantage to take the time to read and clarify it or have an attorney help them with it.

Financial Matters

As an author you are able to deduct from your income taxes certain things you spend money on in order to do your work. These deductions are things like part of your office rent, house payment or rent if you work from home, the cost of office supplies and the equipment you use to do your work such as your personal computers. Check with your tax advisor or use one of the electronic tax calculating services in order to calculate the exact amounts you will be able to deduct.

It's a good practice to keep receipts and very good records of what you spend on things that are necessary to do your work, as well as what your income is, so when tax time comes you will be able to do your taxes or have them done for you with the least effort and get the maximum advantages.

Planning and thinking ahead can save you money. If you wanted to have a party for some influential people and impress them with your new book, you of course want to have the party in as nice a place as possible. If you don't happen to live in a home that costs millions you could of course have your party at a nice hotel. But if it happens that you know someone that does live in a home that's worth millions, and you are on good terms with that person, it might be a good idea to ask the person with the big house if you can have your party at their house. Doesn't hurt to ask, and if the person says yes, you just saved yourself a nice piece of change on the cost of that hotel for the evening. Even if you pay for the use of the house you might be able to save a lot compared to the cost of the hotel.

On the other hand if you happen to have an expensive home and someone asks you if you would be willing to let them use your home for their party, you might want to think about how much they are willing to pay for the use of that nice home, rather than unthinkingly being Mr. Nice Guy and giving away the farm to a bunch of unruly partiers that will enjoy trashing your nice place.

Asking people for favors may sound tacky and absolutely unacceptable to some but to others it's just common business sense, and you may notice in many instances that the people who do it tend to be very well off financially, and maybe as a result of doing it.

Economizing wherever you are able to do so and making a habit of being as financially responsible as possible, can be a big help to you in keeping piece of mind, so your attention is not always fixed on financial problems, leaving you more free to fully concentrate on the writing, publishing and marketing of your books.

Whether your sales commissions are coming from a publisher, bookstore or both, make need to remember to be sure you have set up with them for payment arrangements. They will probably send you an email message to let you know that they need your TIN or tax identification number and your mailing address. If your payer has direct deposit available that is preferable to getting checks in the mail. It's more convenient and safer than mailed checks.

As far as what to do with all those millions you get from your book sales, we will leave most of that for another book, namely a subsequent book to be coming out in the not too distant future, having to do with a checklist of sorts for dealing with Wall Street.

Your Work Just Started

You may be surprised to find if you do not already know, that after finishing your book, the biggest part of your job may have just started.

Providing you are pretty good at writing and have done a good job of putting your book together, you will find that the writing of your book was actually the easy part of your job, and your work has just begun.

If you do happen to know the editor-in-chief of a major publishing firm, or are the nephew of a hot literary agent that continually bats a thousand, or you happen to be a very famous person, then the bulk of your work may in fact already be done. Even then you might still need to keep a close eye on the book sales process to make sure someone at that publishing company does not drop the ball and forget to send out the promotional materials to the bookstores, forgets to sell your book to the bookstores, manages to mess things up in a multitude of other ways or find some other totally original method of completely screwing things up for you. It happens on occasion. People are not perfect and they do make mistakes.

Or you may have completed your book with a good title, with attractive and descriptive covers, now have it in the major bookstores in both print and download and are using the free preview for your book, and find that the sales you are getting are astounding. In this case read no further. Put your feet up, relax and congratulate yourself on a job well done.

But it's all too easy for an author to complete the manuscript, drop it in the mail or upload it to the publisher, get it accepted for publishing, forget about it, start on the next book, and months later find out that nothing is happening with the manuscript. Getting your book in the hands of your readers is often a continual job of paying attention to what is going on with the publishing process and the book sales.

How could that possibly be? It's very simple. The big mega publishing firms operate on the principal of the blockbuster. They have so much money tied up in marketing the books that they really cannot afford to and do not take chances on books that are mediocre.

The mega publisher may have a pile of books sitting there that are very good books, but if they are not completely convinced that those very good books are blockbusters, and will soon be near or at the top of the New York Times Best Seller List, they will not even dream about touching a single one of them. It's simple math. If a large publisher puts a lot of money into marketing a book that flops all that money the publisher invested is out the window, never to be seen again. Even if a book does tremendously well the publisher can come out on the loosing end. If the book brings in ten million dollars and the publisher spent twelve million getting it into the hands of the readers, the publisher is a couple million short.

Given that little tidbit of common sense and practical reality, we must also consider the distinct fact that even if your book is really good and a potential blockbuster, the big publishing houses, in their busy worlds of the blockbuster mentality, made the financial decision to not market your masterpiece. So what do you have to do to get your masterpiece published and get the money from it, and do it without spending more than you make in the process?

Putting up your own money, if you have it or want to and can borrow it, and placing the bet that the big publisher is not willing to place is one answer. The other answer may not be a pretty answer and maybe not something we to think about, but it is nevertheless the answer and I'm afraid it boils down to one simple word which is WORK, and a lot of which you may have to do yourself, whether or not you put up a lot of your own money. But it might not really be all that bad. There may exist some good solutions.

Whether or not your book is ready for prime time on the New York Times Best Seller List, you really want to stay away from the scores of supposedly wonderful literary agents that will be happy to review your book for a substantial fee, and possibly tell you how to fix the book so it is ready for prime time. If your book is blockbuster material the agents that want to charge you those fees probably don't even know any publishers, and wouldn't know one if they saw one. Isn't it wonderful how when you just want to publish and sell your book the nitwits all seem to climb out of the woodwork with their little bottles of snake oil and magic cures that are certain to set you on the road to success?

Author Beware - Publishing Processes To Avoid

Although there are many good agents and publishers there are also those high priced agents and publishers that are not quite so good, and will take your money and not give you much in return. They can be avoided by doing some thorough research beforehand that will save you a lot of grief. If you are unfortunate enough to deal with one of them they will pat you on the head, take you under their wing for a pretty penny, and tell you how you are going to do so well with your book, and hope you don't look at the fine print that explains explicitly how you just screwed up royally, once you sign with them and hand over all that hard-earned cash. You innocently gleam and tell yourself how nice it would be to see your pretty book in print.

That does seem like it would be such a nice first step. But as fate and good luck would have it, you may have just fell off the turnip truck, and you may look like you were born yesterday, but somehow you are just not quite stupid enough to go with that smiling snake oil salesman turned fly-by-night agent or publisher. He would be so glad to take your money and manage to do his best to avoid you and never speak to you again. If he did speak to you again it would only be to tell you to look at all those pretty books of yours that got printed and are so neatly stacked, and tell you to please read the fine print, because he really does not want to explain to you just why it is that all the cash you gave him just somehow didn't manage to sell a single copy of all those books.

Then you look at that fine print on your contract, that you didn't look at in the beginning, which explains to you in detail how the publisher is not responsible for all those books of yours that are so rapidly collecting dust mostly because no one knows they exist.

Or you managed to find a very good publisher with a lot of books out there in the marketplace, and this one is along the lines of a conventional print publisher who sells books to schools and libraries, and he agrees to publish your book. He explains to you how wonderful your book is, how he enjoyed reading it, but also carefully explains that publishing is a risky business and how you will have to share in the risk, which is why he is not paying you any $5,000 or more advance on your book, that you would get from a good publisher if the publisher knew he was holding gold, because he is not really at all sure about the potential your book has of selling.

You do understand about no advance and yet somehow find yourself overjoyed knowing that your book has actually been accepted by the publisher, and will soon be in print. Then after waiting many months you receive a dozen copies of your book, and start counting all that money you will be getting from all those many book sales. After a good many more months of not seeing any royalty checks in the mail, you contact the publisher who tells you that yes, your books are selling, but not in large quantities.

It's good news indeed to hear that there are at least some sales, but you are considerably saddened after the publisher says he will send you the money but never manages to get around to doing that. And all this failure to pay you for all your work on your book boils down to the fact that this publisher is not actually in the same country you are, and does not really have to pay you. You have no legal course of action because the publisher does not live where you live and so once again you are completely screwed.

Or you happen to be the proud owner of a new website for which maybe you paid a lot of money, or developed it yourself with all the do-it-yourself things there are around, and you are unfortunate enough to think that because you now have your new book on the all powerful Internet, also known as the worldwide web, that you have just struck gold. That would be nice if you have enough people visiting your website, but unfortunately, even with the help of the very effective search engines that automatically scan your site every 24 hours or so and catalog your content, you are saddened to find that your book or books just are not selling.

Isn't it nice to know that someday, when the world runs out of firewood, you will be able to come along with all your dusty books and help people keep warm? Could there possibly be a better way to go? Let us hope.

The simple fact is, even if your book is not best-seller material, the reason it is collecting dust could very well be that no one really knows it exists. So now that we completely understand that we can get on with the business of helping people become aware that your book is there, it's a nice book, it will not harm people, and actually is possibly a very good book and may do them a great deal of good by reading it.

Publishing & Selling Checklist

Yes, it's that old idea again of not trying to keep everything in our head, but rather putting it down on paper or in our computing device. Some of us truly have incredible minds, total recall, photographic memories and all those neat kinds of things that our minds can do. And since we have all those good things going for us, let's add to it the step of keeping a checklist, just in case our mind gets a little foggy one day. Following a good checklist will be a great help and keep us from later scratching our heads and telling ourselves, "OMG! I got so busy that I forgot to tell anybody about my book!"

1 - Publisher & Publishing Process Selection – If you have not already done so, decide upon the type of publishing and the publisher that will be best for you and your book – Research different publishers and processes as detailed in Chapter Four to help you in making your decision. √

2 - Manuscript Format – Set up the proper format to be used for submission. √
> A - Conventional publisher – paper submission - Use double-spacing, one-inch margins both sides. Include header at top with title and your name, footer at bottom with page numbers. Use the same font throughout the entire book
> B - Self Publishing or POD (print on demand) publisher – book template format from the publisher, paperback, 6x9, 8.5x11 etc. Ensure margins are correct for printing

3 - Manuscript Contents Outline – √
> A - Fiction
>> Plot Outline - Outline of what will be in your book (for your own use, not for submission)
>> Characterization or description of your main character and other characters
>> Story plot
>> Climax
>> Ending
> B - Non-Fiction
>> Table of Contents
>> Dedication, if wanted
>> About The Author
>> Forward
>> Index

4 - Manuscript Completion Steps √
>> Corrections
>> Formatting
>> Grammer
>> Rewrites

Proofing

5 – Book covers – front & back covers & spine √

Design eye-catching covers with photos or illustrations if wanted and descriptive text that will make people want to buy your book. Design yourself or consult a design expert

6 – Completion & Submission √

A - Mail or submit online all materials, manuscript and book covers to the publisher

B - If you mail a paper manuscript to a publisher use one-inch margins, double spacing, header at top with title and your name and page numbers at bottom, mail loose, no binding of any kind and no staples

C - Submit an application for copyright registration to the Library of Congress at http://www.copyright.gov/

7 – Proof and approve final copy from publisher after submission√

8 – Distribution Process√

A - Make available for Google Book Search

B - Make available for online bookstores by selecting a distribution package

C - Make available for electronic download from bookstores

D - Make online samples or partial free look or previews available

E - Create an Audio version of your book for distribution (Optional) – there is likely a cost to this depending upon the size of your book and if you have a company do it for you. It is possible to do it yourself but labor intensive enough that you may want a company to do it for you – see Audio Books in Chapter Four

9 – Marketing Processes √

A - Name Check – Do a very thorough search of the title of your book and the author's name prior to publication. Make sure your book's title is not the same or close to something that's already being used. Use a Penname for your author's name if necessary to avoid using a common name

B - Make sure your book gets listed with Amazon, other bookstores and Google Book Search

C - Make certain your book is available for download as well as print

D - Check to make sure your book is Preview Enabled with Google Book Search, Amazon and other online bookstores

E - Tags or Keywords – Lookup your book on Amazon, weRead and other bookstores and create keywords and tags so people will be able to easily find your book

F - Press Releases – Do research on press releases to decide what kind to use

G - Create a website if you don't have one, or hire someone to do it – Google and others are free and easy for doing your own website

H - List and display your book on your own website and other places online

I - Put a link to your website or wherever your books can be seen in your outgoing email template

J - Before advertising you book, your website or anything else verify and confirm traffic rankings and reputation of the companies you advertise with - look them up on Alexa.com if they are in the top 100 Advertise online and/or in print

K - Promote through social networking websites - If you use a Penname or psudonym you may want to use it as your name when signing up for the social networking sites, so people will be able to find you and your books

L - If you publish your book with LuLu Publishing your book is automatically in the weRead.com databse. Activate the weRead application on FaceBook and use all the weRead tools you can to make your books available to your friends from weRead

M - Create an attractive business card and hand them out with your phone number and website address to everyone you meet. Never leave home without your business cards

N - Request guest appearances on TV and Radio talk shows

O - Connect with publisher and author blogs and other online discussion groups to increase your exposure and gain knowledge Arrange with brick and mortar bookstores for book releases and book signing events

P - Dress appropriately for book signing events, giving out your business cards or wherever you meet other people, no casual attire, business casual at a minimum, no t-shirt and jeans

Q - Keep a birthday and holiday gift list of everyone you know, friends, relatives, customers, send birthday cards, notes and/or gifts with the address to your website

10 – Sales Commission Processes √

Setup your accounts and make payment method selections to get your sales commissions or royalties from the bookstores and/or publishers. They will probably send you an email message to let you know that they cannot pay you unless they have your TIN or tax identification number and method of payment, with your mailing address or checking account data for direct deposit. Direct deposit is preferable if available. It's more convenient and safer.

CHAPTER THREE

Title & Author's Name

Having your book well listed with the world's biggest bookstores is probably just about as good as it gets. The rest is secondary and can be optional. Notice we said "well" listed. Seeing it in those big bookstores is very exciting, but a good searchable title, in print and download as well, search tags or keywords, nice looking cover with the free preview feature has to go along with it for you to succeed. Without those essentials your book can easily get lost in the crowd and collect a lot of dust on a shelf somewhere or in bookstore cyberspace.

Give your book a good title, something clever, humorous, unique and catchy that people will remember, an attractive cover and pay attention to the author's name. It's very important to do an Internet search and make sure some one else's book does not have the same name. You are able to publish your book if the name is already being used because the name of the book cannot be copyrighted, but it's better for marketing purposes if the name of your book or its title is very unique. Ideally your title should contain words or phrases for which people are already searching. Do your research carefully to find out what is currently popular in searches, and also pick a title that will be popular for as long as possible.

Avoid a title and content that would tend to date your book. This can extend the lifecycle of your book or the length of time it will be popular and will sell. For example, How To Get The Most Fun From a Hoola Hoop. The Hoola Hoop was something that was popular in the 1950ies and has minimal popularity now, unless you are the manufacturer of this item and want to do a revival campaign for it. A dated fiction or non-fiction title such as The Winds of World War One could be okay, the latter being a documentary book. Some books, particularly technical will have a shorter lifecycle than others because technology changes so rapidly. A non-fiction book can be obsolete even before it gets into print, such as a technical book that falls short of covering the latest state of the art subjects that are changing moment by moment, and does not get into print and the marketing arena fast enough.

You can search titles on Google Book Search, Amazon and other online bookstores to make sure a title you have in mind is not already being used. You can use it even if it is already being used because the title cannot be copyrighted, but you may want to do some creative editing to your title that someone else is also using. For example, you could use a subtitle that would help distinguish your book as different from the other one with the same title. But it's better if you use a title that is not at all the same as any already being used.

Some may not think so but your name is also very important. Someone who reads a book you published happens to like it, and they want to see other books written by you and search your name. If your name is John Smith the chances of them finding about the other books you have written is very slim. If you happen to have a very uncommon name you are fine. But do a search on your name and make sure you are the only one who has it or is using it. Rex Lee Reynolds is not my real name. It's a Penname I use because my real name is so common it may as well be John Smith, and that is not good. If you Google my real name you will come up with a politician in Texas who is not nearly as pretty as I am, but does have my name and even my middle initial. You will find ten million people on Google who has the same name as me.

If you do have a common name make up a Penname or pseudonym as they are called. Think of the most unusual name you can so it will stay unusual as long as possible. Use the full middle name to help with the uniqueness.

If the title of your book is unique and your name or your Penname is unique, you have a much better chance of selling your book because it's much easier for people to find you and your book in the bookstores and on the Internet.

Book Covers

The publishers all have book cover design departments or someone that will help you with your book covers. If you are with one of the large mega publishers you won't need to be concerned with the design or the cost of it other than maybe approving it. If you are with a smaller publisher you may need to pay design fees to have the book covers done for you if you don't want to do it yourself. If you do it yourself some of the online POD publishers have very nice online tools you may use to create your book covers at a very good cost if not completely free.

Although it's entirely possible to publish and sell your book with a cover that consists mostly of just text and a colored background, it is better to put some time into making the cover of your book something that stands out from the competition. I prefer to use an attractive photo or illustration on the front cover and maybe another on the rear cover, something that is eye-catching and interesting. Remember that a picture is worth a thousand words. There is an old saying of "don't judge a book by its cover," but you will find that a lot of people do, and if people see your book they may just buy it because you have a nice looking cover, and some good descriptive text on the front and rear covers with colorful backgrounds that briefly and concisely presents the contents.

But don't rely on a photo on your covers alone. Accompany your photos or illustrations with descriptive and exciting text that will make the visitor want to buy your book. Put an attractive description on the front cover, more description on the back cover and maybe a bio of yourself as the author. Very well planned book covers can make a big difference in how people will view your book and a big difference as well in the sales. Look at books in the bookstores to get ideas for your covers.

Submission

Now that your book is ready for publication what's the next step? You submit all the materials for your book to your publisher, the manuscript and covers. Whether you are using a conventional publisher where you mail in your book's materials, or make your submission to a POD publisher, the publisher will let you know your book materials have been received. You will get an ISBN, a unique number that distinguishes your book from all the others on the market. If your book is being marketed with a conventional publisher you will see your ISBN on your published book. A POD publisher will provide you the ISBN with instructions to insert into your book and resubmit the manuscript for publication with your ISBN.

With a POD publisher you should get a final proof copy so you can examine exactly what your readers will get when they see your book in the bookstore or online, and what they see when they buy it or order it online. You approve the final copy after proof reading and making sure it has the ISBN issued to you, and your book is published. And of course, unless you are fortunate enough to have a publisher that is thoroughly convinced that your book is a best-selling blockbuster, this is where your work is just beginning. If a publisher or anyone who sees your book does put it into the category of the blockbusters don't be surprised if you get an offer to buy the rights to your book, someone sends you a large check as an advance or tries to snuggle up to you in a number of ways, because it's business and part of the supply and demand thing that makes everything work.

It can take a few months after initial publication for books to show up on Amazon and Google Book Search. For two books of mine published through LuLu Publishing they showed up on Amazon within two to three months, but in the print version only. Making books available for download with Amazon is a separate process. I submitted the Amazon download version, or Kindle book reader wireless version separately, as well as signing up for Amazon's Look Inside The Book preview feature, which also requires the book covers and the manuscript be uploaded, but it's easy to do and only takes a few minutes. Google Book Search is not automatic either. I had to set that up myself. But these things are relatively easy to setup, we just have to have them on our checklist and make sure to do them manually as part of our book marketing process. Google has mentioned that, like Amazon, as of early 2010 they will also have available the electronic download feature for books listed on their Google Book Search.

The Blockbuster Mentality

We know the mammoth book publishers are diving and digging frantically and looking through their piles of manuscripts to find that one trendy, iconic and unique book that is going to bring them landslide sales and keep them on the profit side of things. Then again, maybe not, maybe they know the entire pile is just firewood and are really just waiting for the manuscripts to arrive in the mail from the movie stars and politicians that don't even need the money. We of course want it to be our book and if we just discovered the cure for some dread disease, just ended our term in the oval office or are the new superstar kid on the block, the success of our book is very much assured.

If our book does not happen to fit into the blockbuster group it can still be a very good book with a lot of potential for sales. It may sell very well or moderately well from the bookstores and yet not get on the bestseller list. We do have to keep in mind that there are an enormous number of good books chasing a limited number of eyeballs. If it is the case where we didn't make it onto the bestseller list we can be content with the sales we get or we can take other steps to increase the sales of our book. There are a lot of bestsellers, quite a lot of them but there are many more books that are not bestsellers that could maybe use some help. If our book needs some help here are some things we can do.

What, No Sales?

As exciting and exhilarating as it is to see your book finally in print and available online in print and download, it is equally as disheartening to realize a few months later that very few or even maybe not a single copy of your book has been sold. And if we look we might find it hasn't been selling simply because very few people or know it's sitting there among millions of other books, many of which are not selling either. So now you go about the business of selling your book. And just exactly how do you do that? This is where we get to the fun part of making people aware that your book is there, that it's for sale if they would like to take a look at it and maybe even buy it.

You Can Handle The Truth

The Ugly Cold Reality of it - This is the part that so many of us really hate when we get introduced to it, the idea of being a salesperson. Or who knows? Maybe this will be your favorite part. Even if you have a lot of money and can pay someone who will do it, maybe you just like selling things. But if you are like many of us you will emphatically tell yourself with a scowl, "I'm not a salesperson, I don't want to sell things! I'm a writer and an author!" And you pull a sour face when saying it because you were under the impression that the masterpiece you wrote should be able to stand on its own and sell many millions of copies without you becoming a door-to-door salesperson.

Welcome to reality my friend. Because even if you do know that editor-in-chief of a major publishing firm or that literary agent that bats a thousand, and they just didn't see a blockbuster in your book, you are now a salesperson, unless you want to put up a lot of money for the marketing of your book. Even if you are pretty well off financially and decided to put up the money, you may find yourself doing at least some of the selling, and you will be sure to keep a close eye on things to make sure your money was well spent.

If your book is doing well in the bookstores, of course you do not have to spend your time in the sales process, but we notice a lot of authors who's books are doing well will also involve themselves in the sales process because they know it results in more sales. To make it easier, just think of it as asking someone to buy your book, because in its simplicity that's what you will be doing.

It's all too easy for any of us to assume that if our book has been successfully distributed to the brick and mortar bookstores and all the online bookstores, that our book will sell, and although it does and can happen, it is just not always the case. For example, if a new book is listed on the world's biggest online bookstores, we could logically think that it's a given that plenty of sales will soon be the result. But unfortunately for so many books there are those times when it just doesn't happen.

With the remarkable technology that exists with tags, keywords, look inside or previews and so many other very useful techniques, if the new book happens to be something that millions of people are searching for this will certainly help tremendously with the book at least being seen, which will increase the chances of sales. But the fact remains that the book will just sit there until the end of time going unnoticed if people are in fact not searching for it. And if those millions of people are not searching for your book, an improvement in the number searching and finding it will be a result of a successful marketing campaign, or a number of them that will follow the publishing of your book.

Book Signing Events

When my first book was published the idea of book signing sessions at bookstores did cross my mind, but very briefly. It was only a thought and a fleeting thought and not something I seriously considered in the least. And I didn't do book signings other than a few copies that I signed and gave to friends. No, I told myself, that's not for me. If I can't just write a book that's good enough that it will sell on its own, then forget it. And of course I have noticed best selling authors doing book signings and promoting their books on TV and Radio talk shows. And I tell myself "thank God I don't know Jay Leno or David Letterman and have no connections that could ever get me on their show. God forbid someone should pull me out of my cave and shove me in front of a camera, which might result in somebody actually buying a copy of one of my books. And besides, I'm just not into it." No way in the world is anyone going to get me in front of a TV camera or on a Radio talk show. So low and behold God does forbid it because as it works out in the end, no one knows me, and no one has the slightest idea that I have written a book.

But fortunately everyone is not as shy as I am and may have nothing against getting in good with the manager of a bookstore, arranging for a book signing event and spending a weekend afternoon or two chatting with the crowd, signing copies of their books and making a lot of new friends in the process. It's done all the time and some make it a big part of their book sales process.

TV & Radio Talk Shows

Okay, so you and I may not be ready for prime-time TV talk shows or Radio talk shows. Or maybe we are and just don't realize it yet. Maybe you are one of the many people who clamor for the limelight. Radio would be easier it seems because there is no camera, but getting an interview seems virtually impossible with all the authors that are willing to do it and are asking for the interviews. No harm in trying though. It doesn't cost anything to ask and only takes a minute or so with an email message to the radio and TV stations.

If you do happen to be able to get on a talk show of some kind and are willing to do it, then that is wonderful. You just may have sold a bunch of your books. But for so many people that's just not going to happen, even if they want it to happen. Looking at it realistically, most of the people we see on the talk shows are already famous, very well known, and on occasion the talk shows will have a newcomer on and give them a chance, depending upon the quality of the book.

If we are willing to be on talk shows there is no harm or anything to lose by trying. Most authors that get on the talk shows already know someone or are invited after someone has noticed their book. But we can at least send an email message to the talk show hosts with a link to our website where the hosts can review our book and let us know if they want us on their show.

When we look at the numbers we can easily see that doing a guest appearance on a talk show is just about as good as it gets. There can be many millions of people who see or hear the show and they will get to know about that great book. Guests are also sometimes paid to be on some talk shows, and who knows? Maybe the guests also get some pretty good food while waiting to go on.

None of this is to say that if you are unable to get on the talk show circuit, you are completely on your own, or that there is no help of any kind available, because there certainly is a lot of help available. The old saying that the harder you work the luckier you get seems to hold true, and we will notice this happening as we strive on in the face of adversity and manage to get lucky along the way.

CHAPTER FOUR

Publishing Processes – The One Best For You

It's always good to have choices, isn't it? It would be a very boring world if there were no choices. The best publishing process for you would depend upon you or what kind of person you are, which we can divide into several types.

If you just finished your book and already have a publisher making out a big advance check and putting it in the mail to you, you already know which publishing process is best for you and don't need to bother with a decision. But if you got a lot of rejection slips from agents and publishers and no interest from any of them, and still want to publish your book, there are some other ways you can go, depending on the kind of person you are.

If you are the hands-on do-it-yourself kind of person who likes to get out the hammer and nails and fix things yourself then self-publishing is probably going to be your thing. If you are not the do-it-yourself type and tend to call the repair guy when something needs to be fixed then you can still do self-publishing but will need a little or a lot more help, and will need to pay more to have your book published. Even if you are the hands-on type and like doing things yourself maybe you are very busy and don't have the time. Whatever the situation there is a solution for everybody.

Conventional Publishing

Conventional publishing consists of getting your book into print by first writing a query letter to a literary agent or to the editor of the publishing company. If the agent or publisher is interested from what you have put in your query letter to them, they will tell you to send your manuscript, or maybe the first few chapters. If the publisher wants to publish your book they will buy the rights to the book from you and pay you a royalty on sales. Depending upon how much confidence they have in your book the publisher may pay you an advance on the royalties. If they are not interested they will send you a rejection slip, briefly telling you they are not interested.

Writers Market has a list of all the agents and publishers who have requested to be on the list. Writers Market is a book with an associated website at www.writersmarket.com. It provides names and addresses of the agents and publishers. Each agent and publisher will state the guidelines in their listing regarding what kind of books or literature they are looking for with specific details as to how they prefer writers to communicate with them. Publishers will also mention in their listings if they accept query letters from writers or only from agents representing writers.

The query letter describes briefly what your book is about, enough to give an agent or publisher some idea if your book is something they would like to know more about. If an agent or publisher likes your letter they will ask you to send your manuscript or a few sample chapters. If your book is accepted for publication you might get an advance from the publisher. The average advance is a few thousand dollars but publishers do not have to offer an advance, and some do not. Many publishers will at least provide the author a few copies of the printed book. Some cheap publishers have stated in the listing that a few copies of the book forwarded to the author will be the only payment the author will receive. For the best authors who are on the best seller list the advance can be in the millions of dollars, sometimes even before the publisher has seen the entire manuscript if the publisher knows the author well enough.

I have written many query letters to agents and publishers, estimated in the hundreds, the results mostly being a lot of rejection slips that came back. But I also managed on a number of occasions to have manuscripts reviewed by literary agents. On two occasions when still quite new as a writer I paid a fee to literary agents, a few hundred dollars, and felt the advice I got from the agents was worth the money. I also had several of my manuscripts reviewed by literary agents at no cost to me, with good advice that was provided. On one occasion a query letter to a conventional publisher resulted in the publisher offering a contract and acquiring the rights to two of my manuscripts that were published.

Self Publishing

Self publishing is different from conventional publishing in that you retain the rights to your book, can get your books published much faster, but you do not get an advance of any kind from a publisher, and do not have the financial backing of a large publisher that is selling your books to the bookstores and doing the marketing campaigns for your books. For the most part the author is responsible for the publishing and marketing costs. With self-publishing you are much more on your own regarding the financing and marketing of your books, but self publishing can be an attractive method to use largely due to the technology that has become available in recent years.

With self publishing an author, in addition to writing the book, is likely to be very involved in the processes of publishing and marketing, such as selecting distribution methods, cover designs, book formatting, and uploading the materials to the publisher's website, and possibly all without ever speaking or dealing directly with anyone at the publishing firm. The author can have a one-on-one relationship with someone at a publishing firm, which can be helpful if needed, if he or she is willing to pay more money. Self-publishing firms will likely have the extra services optionally available on a fee basis.

Author House is an example of a publisher that will provide the one-one-on-one relationship. They have POD service available with many marketing and distribution options and advantages, with an impressive list of titles they have published that have gotten on the best-seller lists and that have also been made into movies. If an author visits the Author House website, leaves an email message an Author House publishing consultant will respond right away, and will be able to answer any questions and provide a great deal of one-on-one assistance.

We could also refer to self-publishing in some cases as co-publishing, where the author works with a publisher to get his books into print and into the marketplace. But self-publishing is the term used most since the author has the major amount of responsibility in making sure his book gets published. The publisher helps a great deal in different ways with available services, but the author has to be very involved in the publishing process, as opposed to conventional publishing where if the author is fortunate his major role after he gets the manuscript accepted by the publisher is starting on his next book.

I have published books both through the conventional publishing and through self-publishing processes. It does of course vary with different publishers, but with the **conventional publishing process my books were in the market place within twenty-four months** after I signed the contract with the publisher. That was in addition to the month or two for the query letter and manuscript submission sequence to take place. There was no advance but there was also no cost to me in dealing with the conventional publisher.

With **self-publishing** through a POD or print on demand publisher I had two book manuscripts in paperback print and available for electronic download sales and in the marketplace with the publisher in **less than five weeks**. The same two books were **in stock on Amazon and listed on Google Book Search within sixty to ninety days**. There was no cost to me for my books that were being stocked and ready to be shipped to the buyers by Amazon. My only cost for self-publishing the two books was for proof copies of the paperbacks that came to **less than twenty dollars per book**.

Vanity & Subsidy Publishers

Let's remember that we never want to assume anything. It's better to find out. Despite some of the damning things we might read about them, it would seem that all vanity or subsidy publishers are not all bad and actually may have a place in the market. If they were all bad no one would be dealing with them, and it could be that some of them are actually very good. Some of the vanity or subsidy publishers have published an awful lot of books, and some with some impressive people as authors. And as far as how many of those books that got printed were also bought by someone, it all comes back again to the very important activity of doing our research before diving in.

You may want to find out more about the vanity publishers or subsidy publishers if it happens that you are a famous person and didn't get a call or letter from that big publishing company that you were expecting. Or if you are very successful in some other way and have not been able to get a major conventional publisher to buy the rights to your book, there may be yet a solution for you. If you have a good amount of money to spend on the publishing of your book, then a vanity or subsidy publisher may be the way for you to go. It may be that you are busy entertaining people in one way or another, your music CD is going platinum, or your many business activities keep you on the road a great deal, and the big conventional publisher neglected to contact you or your business manager about a book deal. You don't have the time it takes to do the kind of hands-on self-publishing that is lower cost but will take quite a lot of your time. If this is the case maybe you could use a good vanity or subsidy publisher to get your book into the market and make you some money from it. But no matter how busy you might be you will still need to invest some time to do research on the publisher before signing with them, or have someone do it for you. Use your own judgement based upon the information you get when making your decision.

When doing your research use common sense and look for things that do not add up or don't make sense. If it looks or sounds too good to be true it probably is. One of the advantages we have with the online world these days is the review process. When we buy something we are often asked to write a review on the item that we bought, and we can many times read the reviews of others before making the decision to complete the purchase. Take a look at the data or information that is presented and decide if it adds up and makes sense. If it does add up and makes sense look around for reviews on the company from where you got the information, and see what others have to say about it.

If you are able to find information from another source about a vanity or subsidy publisher in the way of a review or complaint, compare it with information from people who have done well with the publisher. You won't have to ask for references. The publisher will be sure to mention the testimonials from happy authors. But there's nothing to say that you cannot think outside the box and confirm some of those testimonials, just as you would if you were hiring an employee. Confirm what the publisher is telling you in their sales pitch by contacting an author or two who have used this publisher and get their story. It can be well worth the time spent.

In talking with someone who is bent on getting their book in the hands of one of the big conventional publishers, or someone very biased towards the less costly hands-on self-publishing, we could get the idea from them that the vanity or subsidy publishers are all con artists that only exist to cheat people out of their money, which may not at all be the case with some of them. Finding out for ourselves would be a better way to go, rather than listening to rumors or complaints of someone that might just be a crackpot, who will never publish a book under any circumstances, because no one would ever want their bum book. And finding out for ourself may consist mostly of making a phone call or sending an email message or having someone do it for us.

If things check out and you're convinced that a vanity or subsidy publisher will do a good job for you, and you are pretty well off financially and would like this kind of service it is certainly there for you. But if you find some holes in someone's story and things do not checkout, or you have very limited funds you may want to consider investing some of your time, paying a lot less with possibly just as much potential of your book selling. If you are the very successful entertainer or busy business person without much spare time, and find that the story does not check out with the vanity or subsidy publisher, you can hire someone to put some time into the less costly kind of publishing that can get the job done for you.

Print On Demand Publishers – PODs

If we have decided that we are the kind of person who is the hands-on type, has sufficient time and would like to publish our book in a low cost manner, we can go with a print on demand self-publisher. We can get our book in print and available for electronic download by using a good POD publisher such as LuLu Publishing at www.lulu.com, the publisher through which this book has been published. LuLu does not charge anything to create an account with them and many of their services are free. They have a generous 80/20 author publisher split on the book reciepts.

There are other POD publishers around if you would like to look for them. I used LuLu for two previous books, Closet Full of Teddy Bears and Trouble in Sleepy Springs, and found LuLu to be an excellent publisher to use for a very good many reasons. I am not associated with LuLu Publishing in any way other than being an author that uses their services. LuLu Publishing is not paying me for an endorsement.

My two previous books that were published with LuLu are now in stock on Amazon.com, referred to as the world's biggest bookstore, and the only cost to me was ten or fifteen dollars for the paperback proof for me to approve that came from the publisher. I didn't pay a dime for the books that are in stock at Amazon. That looks to me to be a far better deal than paying thousands to have an expensive publisher print books for me that maybe no one is going to see or likely never even know about. Then again, if you're not the do-it-yourself type or don't have the time but have some money, maybe it's worth paying a pretty good price to get your books published, and maybe included in what you will pay will be some good marketing that will turn into sales.

Advantages of POD Publishers

LuLu and other POD publishers have a great many tools and features that can be a big help in formatting your book, submitting it, obtaining an ISBN, getting your book listed in all the book databases and getting it published. There are many tutorials and loads of informational help sections that will answer just about any question you will have about what to do with your book in order to get it into the proper format for publishing, including templates for various book sizes like paperback, hardcover etc. There is a cost calculator you can use to determine the exact retail prices, costs and royalties.

POD publishers have features available to help you with the marketing and selling of your books. There are various distribution packages that range in price from free to a few hundred dollars or more. Dealing with an POD publisher can be a very productive and exciting experience but is certainly not a cureall where we push a magic button and have everything done for us. We do have to write a good book that will sell, then use the correct tools to sell it. It's a lot of work but what isn't? Things are always changing everywhere and a POD publisher is no different, and if we're with a good publisher those changes will probably be in the form of improvements. There's always a lot to learn for beginners and veterans alike, but it's wonderful they are on the Internet for us to access and utilize. With a little time and effort on our part we can find POD publishers to be a great deal of help to us and convenient storehouses of very valuable knowledge.

POD Distribution Methods & Choices

It may be possible to select a distribution package at no cost, which will allowed an author to get books onto Google Book Search and Amazon within a few months of initial publication. I did this with Lulu Publishing. It can be exciting to know that for no charge people will be able to find and review your book on Google Book Search and buy it on Amazon, as well as from the publisher in both paperback and via download, download normally being lower in price, depending upon what you set the price at. Google has added an electronic download services as well as of early 2010.

There are also distribution packages for reasonable prices that can be very advantageous. If you are willing to pay for a distribution package your book can also be put into book databases that will make your book available to other bookstores in addition to Amazon, such as Barnes And Noble, Borders and B. Dalton. It's up to the bookstores as to if they want to stock your book, but your book will be listed in the database for the bookstores to examine and make their decisions. As to the costs of the distribution packages it would be best to create an account with a POD publisher to find out, if you have not done so already. And you can create an account with more than one for comparison purposes.

Speaking of distribution methods, not to be confuesed with distribution packages, we don't want to overlook the electronic downloadable versions that are gaining in popularity. E-books or electronic books did not initially do well because readers like to read something they can hold in their hands, but this problem has been solved with the coming of the popular book-reader devices. More and more books are being made available for downloading as an option to purchasing more expensive paperback, hardcover or other print sizes. Buyers can pay for the e-book, for which the cost is usually less than print version and can be reading it almost immediately. The paper print versions from bookstores or print on demand from publishers take a few days for the buyer to get it in the mail. The download version price can be set at whatever you want and are usually less than print because no paper is used. For example an e-book might be about $5 as compared to the paperback version for maybe $12 or so depending upon the size of the book.

It is estimated that the downloadable books have reached about 35% of the online market as of fall 2009. If you get your books listed on Amazon it is quite easy to also add them to Amazon's Kindle book reader section for electronic download. The other online bookstores also have book readers available as well. I did this with my two books and the procedure for doing so with Amazon was quite easy. The download versions include a text-to-speech enabled feature, so readers can also listen to the books. The electronic download versions on Amazon can be downloaded to the iPhone and iPod Touch as well as the Amazon Kindle reading device, and it stands to reason that the other cell phone manufacturers will likely add the book reading features to their cell phone models. As of November 2009 there are about 350,000 titles in the Amazon Kindle section. The number of book readers in use doubled in 2009 and is expected to double again in 2010.

Downloadable Versions And E-Books Are Not The Same

It can be easy to confuse an e-book with a downloadable version of a paper book. You can mistakenly be under the impression that if your book is available for download it is an e-book. They are not at all the same thing. When someone purchases a download version they get your book in an Adobe Acrobat PDF file format. The difference is in the formatting. Downloading a book in PDF format for reading on a PC or Mac is technically a great deal different than reading it on an electronic book reader, cell phone or other wireless device. An e-book is formatted differently for various distribution methods that exist, and it's a separate process entirely from simply making your books available for download in PDF.

For example if you look at one of my paperback books on the LuLu website in my storefront you will see a link next to the paperback book that says, "also available in download." If this same book has not been put through the e-book formatting and creation process, when you search for the same title under E-books you will not be able to find it. Formatting your book for e-book distribution will give you an extra marketing advantage since it will be available for many more distribution channels when put into e-book format.

Your publisher will have information available to you on their website as to how you can create an e-book version of your book for greater distribution advantages.

Great strides have been made in the wireless industry in the last few years with cell phones, iPods and the like, and we can expect the advances to continue. The electronic bookreaders are now coming out with new models that no longer display the pages in only black and white text. They are now capable of downloading and displaying to the readers color illustrated books with photos, videos and whatever we might be able to imagine.

It's important to remember that even if you select a distribution package that makes your books available to all book outlets, it is still no guarantee that your books are going to sell. You have to publish and distribute a good book, one with a good title, unique author's name and excellent contents that people will be searching for in the bookstores and online.

Second & Subsequent Editions

For that non-fiction book that is selling quite well you may likely want to consider going through it and making some improvements for a second edition. Don't get so engrossed in your next book that you forget the second and subsequent editions of the one that's selling. If your book continues to be popular and gets lots of sales you may find yourself doing more than a second edition, which of course will help keep the sales going for as long as possible. It could easily be that things that have changed since you first published your book and an update would be good. We know things never stay the same, change is continually happening and there does not seem to be any absolutes as far as achieving perfection. An update may be needed after a few months and some good improvements may be possible.

Audio Books

Audio books have been popular for quite some time and are another option for additional sales if you want to pay to have your books distributed in audio format. It's quite possible to create and market the audio version yourself if you have the time, but you may want to consider having a company do it for you if you can afford it. There are a number of companies that will convert your book to an audio book, and some with software you can get to help you do it yourself. One such company that may be able to help you with this is Hudson Audio at http://www.hudsonaudiopublishing.com. If you do a search you will likely find a number of other companies as well that are in the business of creating and marketing audio books.

Tech Support & Help

If you have never had dealings with a publisher, conventional or otherwise it's good to know beforehand that when dealing with one it's not always a situation where you can call them on the phone with questions, or even email them and expect to get a swift reply. If you are able to get the one-on-one kind of service you can expect to pay for it in one way or another. Like most companies of all kinds that are online the many of the publishers may have quite limited if not any helpdesk resources, in regards to humans who answer the phone and help customers resolve their problems.

Other than the computer manufacturers that have tech-support people who answer the phone, most online companies largely expect their users to rely on the interactive help systems that are on their websites. Even the companies with people manning the phones use the live tech-support as a last resort, and will at first in a phone recording refer you to their websites. With today's web technologies we are more than ever expected to use the self-help systems on websites as much as possible.

If you read some of the blogs (web logs) of POD publishers you may notice some authors complaining that they can't get anyone on the phone and cannot get their emails answered. When seeing these complaints it would seem understandable to some that it would only be reasonable for customers or authors to be able to get their questions answered and their problems resolved, but in looking at this a little closer we most certainly find that a very large percentage of the answers to the user's questions have already been answered on the publisher's website in the help section, if the user would take the time to look it up. For it to make better sense it can be good if we look at what the complainers are paying for the support they want, which is not much if anything at all.

To some of us it could seem like there are no people anymore, just computers and gadgets that are running everything, which to some degree is probably true, with us hoping they are running it well. And since it is becoming more and more this way, we have to adjust to it and utilize as much as we can the computers and gadgets that are gradually taking the place of the humans. Unless we are willing to pay a lot for support that we might find ourselves seldom using, it's starting to seem like God and websites help those who help themselves.

So much of what we do these days whether we are a writer or not depends upon the technical world in which we live. Maybe you're a wiz at the technical stuff. If you are you are among the very blessed. If you're not someone who breezes through the technical problems without batting an eye, and tend to be among those of us that pull our hair out in frustration, you might want to do what you would do if you have an older car that needs a little attention once in a while.

Knowning that old mechanic that can tell you what's wrong with the car just by listening to the engine, and who can fix it before you have time to have a cup of coffee is a very good person to know. Likewise in the technical world if you are not an ace at fixing the technical things, it's good to know someone who works in an I.T. department somewhere and keep them as a good friend.

CHAPTER FIVE

Marketing Processes

Although none of the subjects mentioned in this chapter will likely be a deciding factor by themselves in your success, but they each have their merits and can play an important part in the overall dynamic scheme of things depending upon how well they are utilized.

At this point let's suppose that you have been successful at publishing your book, not selling it just yet but publishing it, getting it into print and available for electronic distribution. Nobody knows it's there, but it is, at least you know it is because you looked, even if maybe no one else looked. You got the formatting down, maybe used a template from your POD publisher that was very helpful to you in formatting your book with the correct margins and so forth, you got your paper proof copy back from the publisher, and your book is now in print, available for purchase in electronic download format, and listed with all the big bookstores, online and off, depending upon what distribution package you decided upon.

Maybe in addition to being sucessful at publishing your book, you also notice that you have book royalties coming to you from the sales of your book, so much that you don't have time to even count all the money. If this is the case then you need not read any further. Pack your bags, get on your private jet, take off for that remote exotic tropical island you just bought and have a wonderful time. We'll see you when you get back. But if the sales are not happening for you just yet, or the sales are small in number, you may want to stay with us for a while on this and see where we can go from here.

Making Your Book Stand Out From The Crowd

Now we have come to the point where we need to go about the business of letting people know that your book is desirable and available for purchase at their favorite bookstore. Let's keep in mind that at this point no one, or very few if any know about our book. Yes, it is in all those bookstores but we don't know that anyone is looking for it, and should presume that they are not. We need to let people know about our book and want to somehow make it stand out from the crowd.

One of the best examples we could probably think of for something standing out from the crowd is Guy Fieri from the Food Network, who got number two on the New York Times Best Seller List with his book Diners

Drive-Ins & Dives. His book not only stands out from the crowd by the very nature of it, but in fact makes a pretty noticeable amount of commotion, where it tells about him touring the country visiting dozens of restaurants and the many cooking experiences.

Here's a person who in order to stand out and get selected to be on the Food Network in the first place, dyed his hair white, wears funky clothes, has tattoos, developed a number of interesting catch phrases and is a complete bundle of energy. If you or I were to do that we would probably be labeled as a lunatic and get locked up somewhere. But it worked for wonderfully for him along with his also being a such a very nice person that everyone simply adores.

If we look around we can find quite a number of other examples of those who became very well known by doing things to stand out from the crowd. So we know that it does take something different to accomplish that goal. We don't necessary have to jump onto a stage, stand on our head and dance on our hands while holding our book in our teeth, but we likely will need to do something to get the book noticed that is out of the ordinary and probably well off the beaten path. And along those lines we of course want to keep in mind the title of our book, the author's name, the book cover designs and advertising slogans and catch phrases.

Using Humor In Your Writing & Marketing

If you are the kind of person that routinely makes people laugh or has the ability to do so, you already have a great tool working for you, and probably will not overlook the laughter as a powerful tool. It can work both ways. If people think you, your jokes or things you do are funny it warms them up, whether it's something you say or something they read on your book cover. But if you are not into humor and people don't laugh when you tell a joke it's maybe best to stop the bad imitations of your boss or in-laws and not to go the comedian route.

Although it's not for everybody if we think about it we will probably remember some of the most sociable people we have known who would tell a joke here or there and be the life of the party. You may recall knowing a popular coworker or a sales person who always seems to do well in their work and social life, and when you think of them you remember how they keep people laughing by coming up with a good joke here and there or doing something humorous.

It's been being used since the beginning of time. Many of the funniest people in the entertainment world have made millions after learning the mechanics of humor, struggling to the top and telling jokes about how tragic and miserable their lives have been. If it's not something that comes easy for you it may be possible for you to learn the mechanics of humor and develop ways of putting humor into your writing. But if it's too much of a strain or the development of things that are funny take too much of your time, or you are writing for an audience where it would be inappropriate, then best not to use it.

When using humor we must also realize that there are those people who will never laugh at anything, no matter how funny it is, and they are so stone faced that just about everything is inappropriate to them, even if they are not your boss or in-laws that you were unsuccessfully imitating.

The most successful entertainers will tell you that no matter how funny they are, no matter how good their material is, they never expect to win over everyone in the audience. The best of them are satisfied to win over maybe 80 or 90% of the audience, that are hopefully laughing so hard it will drown out any sarcastic or heckling remarks from the few stone-faced critical ones.

Marketing Budget

If it turns out that we are not going with a conventional publisher who is in love with our book and has just sent us that big advance check, we have to ask our self at this point, "just what is the budget I have available for the marketing of my book?" You could say, "Well, I actually have no budget." And if this is the case you will need to immediately look around, check in the piggy bank, cookie jar and create that budget. You will need to decide from the income you have and the money you have saved and other assets if you have any, what are you able to set aside for the marketing and promotion of your book. Since we didn't get the big advance check from the publisher that is not going to spend millions marketing our book, it has to come from somewhere.

Public Relations Firms & Ad Agencies

If your book marketing or advertising budget is healthy enough, and you are confident that you really have an excellent book, you can hire a PR firm or Ad Agency to do all the marketing for you. I will not be able to recommend a PR firm or Ad Agency since have never used one, but your publisher may have some good recommendatios for you, and it's an option you have if you have the budget for it. There are a lot of companies around that can do an excellent job for you. The self-publishing companies have a number of marketing plans, many of which include people or firms for hire that specialize in the marketing of books. If the budget you have decided upon for the marketing of your book is not large enough to hire an ad agency or PR firm there may yet be some other ways to go.

Business Cards

What? You're going to sell your books by standing on a street corner and handing out business cards? No, not at all, but it doesn't hurt anything in the least to have very good looking business cards and give them to everyone you meet. When you meet someone new they may ask what you do, and you can hand them your card. Sometimes it's the little things that can make a big difference. When meeting someone new we know little about them, who they are, what they do and who they know, and they could possibly be someone who might be good to have as a contact.

Whatever your budget is the first thing you need to do is take a few dollars from it and get some business cards. This is the first step. When you have your business cards make a firm rule to never leave home without them. You can leave home without your car keys, your watch, cell phone or your clothes, but don't ever leave home without your business cards. Don't even walk into the front yard or onto the balcony of your home, or anywhere that you might possibly encounter someone.

Do not step outside your door without your business cards. If you do you will invariably run into someone you could have given a card to, and miss a chance to sell one of your books. When you talk to people about your book and you do not have a card to give them, unless you are talking to someone with a photographic memory, which most people do not have, you could easily be completely wasting your time. If the person is very sharp they may memorize what you tell them, but don't count on it.

Design a very nice looking business card with an attractive photo or design on it and something catchy with which people will instantly be impressed. Along with the catchy phrase, attractive photo or design, your phone and fax numbers you will of course want the address to your website or a website where your book can be seen. The printer can also put a message on the back of the card for you at an additional cost. But if you want to leave the back blank you can print a message on the back with the little labels that come thirty on a page, three across and ten down. It takes a little time to print the labels and put them on the back of your cards, but allows you to have a different message from time to time if you want. Vista Print has a very nice web interface for designing your own business cards as well as postcards, calendars and a number of other items at reasonable costs.

Although it's true that many people will throw your card away, or never look at it again after putting it in their pocket, some will look at it, look at your website or the website where your books are for sale, and some will buy your books. The percentage of responses may be low, but it's possible to get a fair amount of responses by handing out your cards. The percentage of responses you will get can be surprisingly good, depending upon how well your card is designed and whether or not you took the time to make some conversation with the recipient, as opposed to just handing them the card and walking away.

Dress Code

Dress code? Are you serious? Is there a dress code for writers? Yes, there is and it's very important, something that should be included in our work habits. The way you dress when writing or doing some of the publishing work on your book is not of great importance, but when you are talking to people in person it is of vital importance that you dress to impress. You don't have to make a fashion statement with elaborate or outlandish looking clothes, best to just come across as pleasant. Business casual attire at a minimum will keep a good impression of you in people's minds. When handing someone your business card or signing books for people at a bookstore, or just about any time you deal with people in person you want to make as good an impression as possible.

How we feel about ourselves is affected by how we dress. If we dress well we feel better about ourselves and it shows in our attitude and the general overall way we come across to other people. People treat us differently when we dress well. They treat us better when we dress well. If you don't believe this you can easily do an experiment with it and find out for yourself. Dress nicely one day and in jeans and a t-shirt the next and pay attention to how people act toward you on the two different days. You will see quite a notable difference.

Sorry if you like to be fashionable and wear the t-shirt and jeans or baggy pants that are way down below your underwear, but a coat and tie for everyday attire for the guys and a nice dress for the girls is not over doing it. For the guys a nice shirt and pants and tie will do nicely for most occasions, and a dress or nice blouse and pants for the girls. The guys can get away with no tie if they wear a nice shirt and pants, but that's about the limit.

Under no circumstances talk to people when you are wearing the jeans and t-shirt, which makes the impression in the minds of people that you really are somewhere below average. When your book is on the best-seller list and you are the talk of the town, you can then wear the t-shirt and jeans if you want, with your jeans fashionably hanging down below your underwear, if you want, and get away with it, but until then you always want to make as pleasant and professional an impression as possible with all the people you meet.

Birthday And Gift Lists

This is something we want to be sure to included in our social networking activities and work habits. It's a helpful, inexpensive and easy way to get and keep the attention from people we know. Keep a birthday list and make sure everybody on the list gets a happy birthday greeting from you in one way or another. Most of the social networking sites keep a birthday list of your friends and fans for you, if you friends and fans enter their birthday, which most of them do. Depending upon your budget you can send birthday cards, e-cards or even just an email, text or instant message note telling them happy birthday, which helps a great deal in keeping you in their minds.

With your friends that you know the best you can send them a signed greeting card, if you happen to have their regular postal mailing address. You may be able to find greeting card companies online that allow you to personalize very attractive cards that you can have mailed to people by regular mail. Your list of friends on your social networking site probably do not have their postal mailing address displayed for you to use, but some do list their email addresses that you can use for quite attractive and sometimes humorous birthday and other kinds of electronic greetings. If someone does not display his or her email address it's probably possible that you can post a link to the electronic birthday card on his or her profile page of the social networking site.

JibJab Greeting Cards & Movies

If you haven't already you will find a very nice selection of electronic greeting cards online, such as American Greetings and others to help you with this task. There are also greeting e-card companies that have a very good selection of very amusing cards that can be customized with photos of you, your friends and family and so forth, such as www.JibJab.com. JibJab also has very humorous movies that you can customize with photos of your head and your friend's heads, then email them to your friends or post the movies on the profile page of your social networking website.

To people you know who are influential to any degree a gift for the birthday and during the holidays can also be a good tool to leverage the amount of attention you get.

Your Website

Now your book is published with an excellent distribution plan, you have it listed in the bookstores with the attractive title, covers and uncommon author's name, it's available in download and print, viewers can preview inside your book, you've selected the good tags and keywords that will help people find it, it's on your website, you've talked it up and plugged it on the social networking sites, everything is ready to go.

Although you may want to work into your budget a plan for your own website if you don't already have one, it may be possible to get one for free if you look around. If you would rather create your own you can easily get by with an inexpensive website. They are much less than they were ten or fifteen years ago, particularly if you do it yourself, which is not really difficult with available technology.

If you are not able to do it yourself or do not want to do it yourself, there are a lot of web developers around that can do it for you. I have developed a number of websites and do my own, with a focus on putting as little time as possible into the development and maintenance of it, so I have as much time as possible left for writing. You may see my website as an example at www.momentsofmagicphoto.com. Even though a lot of work has gone into my website I would be the first to say that it still needs some work, since I focus most my time on writing, but I was happy to find that it got a rating of 7 when submitting it to HubSpot's WebSite Grader free service at www.hubspot.com.

It is not at all necessary to have your own website in order to sell your books, but you will notice that most authors do because it's an additional tool that can effectively help get the word out, and it is easier than ever to create an online presence on the Internet with your own website.

If you want to develop and maintain your website yourself but do not want to use a company with readymade design templates, and want to do the design work yourself, you will need a hosting service, the company that manages the servers where your website and data will be stored. You can do self hosting by getting your own web server, but it is much more cost effective to rent space from a hosting service, unless you have a very large website with visitors to your site that number in the millions.

There are many good hosting services avaiable. They can be searched and compared. I have used a half dozen different hosting services over the years. The one I have used for about the past five years is PowWeb at www.powweb.com. Powweb's rates are very good and they have good tutorials for the beginner and excellent tech support by phone, email or online chat. All hosting services will also include log files that keep a record of the number of visitors to your website as well as a number of other valuable marketing statistics. For example, it's very good to know how long the visitors stay on your website as well as which of the pages are visited the most. If the average time on your site is thirty seconds, this would tend to let you know some changes would be in order to get people to hang around a little longer than thirty seconds and hopefully buy something.

An easier route to go would be web services that provide readymade design templates, that will save you a lot of time and work because you don't have to do the design work. Google Sites, for example is an excellent option for creating your website, and an option as well that is good for people who want to be involved as little as possible with web development, particularly the design part of it, since a great deal of the design work is already done with the readymade page templates. They have a free website creation service in their array of many services, which also includes Google Analytics that will track the traffic to your website and provide you with many valuable statistics.

If you happen to recently have created your first online presence with your own website, don't panic if you one day notice that it is not working quite as it should or is not working at all. All websites go down on occasion, although rarely. Oftentimes in the middle of the night maintenance is being done, but things can and do happen in the middle of the day as well that could cause your site to be offline for a while. If that happens the technical people at the hosting service or wherever your website is located will be working on the problem immediately to get it fixed as soon as possible.

You will notice with some of the biggest companies in the world their website or certain functions of it, may not be working in the wee hours of the morning when maintenance is being done. Many of them will post a notice for you to see when the maintenance is being performed. If you notice your website down you may be able to log into the home page of your hosting service and will probably see a notice explaining why there are problems. You may also be able to email the hosting service or communicate with them via online chat. With a good hosting service you can expect about a 95% amount of uptime.

Your website can be as simple or as elaborate as you want, and will list your book or books with colorful and attractive photos of them and descriptions, with links to where your visitors can purchase your books at various bookstores. By using tags and keywords on your website the Internet search engines such as Yahoo and Google will automatically find your website and books, and will list them in their indexes.

The search engines will look at your site every twenty-four hours or so to pick up any changes you have made. But as good as the search engines are we must keep in mind that having your books listed on your website is in no way a complete marketing solution that will sell your book. Your website is simply an Internet location that you list on your business cards and everywhere else you can think of to list it, in order to get people to see your books, preview them and order them.

Particularly if your website has been up for only a short time, it's very easy to assume incorrectly that because your books are listed on your website and with the search engines that your books will be selling. It's important to pay attention to the amount of traffic or number of visitors that go to your site, and if that number is low some advertising of your site of various kinds can help bring more visitors. Keeping an eye on the traffic statistics or number of visitors to your website will be helpful to you in determining how much your website needs to be advertised.

Email Marketing

Not to be overlooked as a method of keeping in touch with your customers or potential customers is the useful and effective method of email marketing. Each page of your website should have a link to invite your visitors to join your mailing list. If you sell books or other items or services directly from your website you should keep an email list of people who have bought your book, product or service or who have made an inquiry via email.

Anyone who has communicated with you for any reason through your website's email feature will be on your Email Marketing list, which allows you to include them in your bulk e-mailings. You can send periodic updates, newsletters and the like to this list of customers or potential customers, but you must provide an opt-out option so people on your list can ask to be removed from the list. Otherwise you will have problems by becoming labeled as a Spam operator who sends unsolicited bulk email, and will likely have your website hosting services cut off due to complaints from people getting unwanted email from you. Each bulk email you send must have an opt-out explanation at the bottom of the page with a link for people to click that will allow them to make their request and be taken off the list.

If you have a large list you may want to invest in some software that can help you with this. Constant Contact and Send Studio are two such companies with very professional software to help you with managing the marketing to your bulk email list. I have used both these services and prefer Send Studio, but both are good and have very nice templates you can use for your bulk email campaigns and newsletters. The software from both these companies provides an opt-out link on all their templates. The software is very nice, can be customized with your name or your company's name and makes you look very professional.

If you don't yet have a large number of customers and their email addresses there is no need to invest in the bulk email software just yet. You can get by with using your own email program, which will require that you manually remove people from the list that have opted out. Be sure to use the BCC or blind carbon copy feature, which allows you to send your message to a group of people without any of them seeing the email addresses of the rest of the group. Also be sure to put the opt-out option and link at the bottom of your email, and be sure to remember to take people's email addresses off the list that make the opt-out request.

Bundle Marketing

We notice with many things being sold the bundling method is in use. When people buy something they like to think they are getting a lot for their money. When you see an item being advertised on TV for example, do you ever see the item being sold by it self? Rarely if ever will we see anything being sold by it self. The seller will almost always throw in a set of pots and pans with the food chopper to help with the buy-now process and convince the buyer they are getting the best deal they have ever seen. And it's that way with so many other items as well because it makes sense and seems to work.

There is no reason why this cannot be done with book sales as well, and we often see a note in the bookstores mentioning how people who bought this book also bought another or a bunch of others. With many items we often see the two-for-one offer, buy one and get a second free. If you have two or more books available you can perhaps bundle them together with the two-for-one packaging idea, or use another inexpensive but attractive item for free with the sale of the book, or offer the book with the sale of another item. There are many combinations of bundling we can do that is limited only by our imaginations. Always do the bundle sales approach when you can in order to increase they buyers desire.

When sending a book manuscript to a publisher a few years ago the publisher cleverly pointed out to me that I had two books in one, and suggested separating the books, cover more territory and increase the chances of overall sales. The title I submitted was How To Harness The Power of The Internet. The publisher said to cut it into two books, so I did with the second title Web Development As A Business. Being the first books I had published the making of two books from the one had not even occurred to me. The publisher with much more experience spotted it right away and used some smart marketing by having me make two books out of one.

For marketing purposes with non-fiction books writers may want to keep in mind that it might be better to write a number of small books or a series of them rather than one large book. Each small book will cost less than the large book and may result in more overall sales profit rather than offering one large and highly priced book.

Inbound Internet Marketing

HubSpot

You may have noticed the websites of some or even many authors are very simple and nothing at all elaborate, which may very well be all they need, something that displays their books with links to the bookstores. But there is nothing at all wrong with making a few improvements. Anything can be improved and one thing we all want to improve about our website is the number of visitors.

The amount of traffic or number of visitors to your website, as well as sales and leads generated from your website depends upon a number of different factors, many of which are under your control. HubSpot is a company with an impressive staff, most or all from M.I.T. and is a software company with Internet Marketing software available to help you and/or your marketing team to get the most from your online presence. They have a demonstration they give to qualifying companies and periodic webinars (web seminars) that are quite comprehensive and informative.

One does not need to be with a large company to attend the webinars. A company consisting of one employee is fine. I have attended two of their very informative and free webinars. Their first one gave a very good overview of what can be done with the software they have to offer, with a lot of good ideas presented. The second webinar dealt for the most part with how businesses are leveraging FaceBook to assist with their marketing, since FaceBook has had such phenomenal growth in the past few years and is such a powerful resource. The second webinar mentioned FaceBook business or Fan Pages with a lot of tips on how these pages can help a business grow. And HubSpot has Grader Tools for grading the value of a business or fan page at http://facebook.grader.com/ with important tips and suggestions on how to make improvements.

Depending upon the amount of resources you want to put into marketing your website and capitalizing on your online presence, you may want to consider HubSpot at www.hubspot.com to assist you and/or your marketing team with your marketing activities. If you are just starting with the marketing of your books it may be over doing it to spend money on marketing software of any kind, but it won't hurt a thing to become familiar with what is available and very possibly pick up some good information and helpful tips in the process.

HubSpot also has available a free website re-design kit for people who want to enhance their websites for marketing effectiveness. A number of useful items are included in the kit, such as a free Website Grader that will analyze your website when you enter the web address of your site or URL.

The Website Grader is a very useful tool. I was amazed when entering the URL for my website and instantly got back information on what improvements needed to be made to my website in order to bring more visitors. You are able to bookmark or save the Website Grader report for your website, so you can compare it to a new report after making the suggested improvements to your website.

HubSpot also has FaceBook Grader at http://facebook.grader.com/ that will give you a free comparison rating on your fan or business page on FaceBook. It's very easy to use and provides suggestions for improving the performance of your fan or business page on FaceBook. HubSpot also offers a free trial on their marketing software that includes tracking tools.

Press Releases – Talk Shows

When you publish your book you may want to consider a press release or a number of them to help quickly get your book known. The press release can be created in a number of formats that vary in price from free to many thousands of dollars. Most publishers would be able to help you with tips and advice for press releases. The help section of LuLu.com and other self-publishers are good places to learn more about press releases. And there is the idea of TV and Radio talk shows. It may be difficult to get on a TV or Radio talk show in order to plug your book, but you have nothing to lose by trying, and if you get lucky and get on a show, there should not be any cost to you, and in some cases a talk show may even pay you for the guest appearance.

No matter what marketing method is used, be it handing out your business cards, your website, press releases or talk shows, it is certain that there will be a lot of work involved. To give us an idea about the talk shows for example, there was a lady a few years ago who did the talk show circuit to promote her book on sex therapy, supposedly a popular subject. During one of her best years her book grossed over half a million dollars. Over a period of quite some time she did several thousand of the talk shows. That's a great deal of work but she was willing to do it in order to get the sales.

Talking To People

To get into effective sales of a book it might be good if we look at a politician's attitude about the whole matter of gaining acceptance. In order to get elected they find themselves most effective when they get out, knock on every door in the neighborhood and press the flesh, as they call it, or meet people and shake hands with them, with the old eye-to-eye contact that helps them make the sale.

Many of us would tend to talk to people as a second nature or do it automatically without the need for giving much thought to it. We would probably do that at least to some degree by giving a business card to people we encounter wherever we go away from our office. If someone is a little shy it would be easy to have a bad habit of only handing the card to someone and walking away. It's much more effective to also talk to the person, shake their hand and ask their name, and engage in a bit of conversation, which increases the chance that they will like us, remember us and possibly sooner or later buy one or more of our books.

Advertising

It should be easy for anyone to see that there is a great deal of waste involved in much of the advertising that we see all around us. Advertising can be and most times is very expensive and often brings back a low ROI or return on investment. It's important to consider very carefully what kind of advertising you want to do and with what firm or firms.

Probably the lowest cost type of advertising is what was just described, the personal contact, when you happen to be around other people and hand them a business card and make some small talk with them, which hopefully results in the all powerful word of mouth happening. If you sell someone on your book the person will likely tell their friends about it, particularly if they like it after reading it. But as well as being low cost the personal contact kind of advertising is relatively low volume and time consuming, something we definitely want to do but mostly as a social habbit, in addition to some professional advertising that would probably involve some good automation to be successful.

Our advertising objective should be to effectively get the message out in volume, and by effectively we would mean to the correct target market. You might want to consider advertising your website, at least a minimum amount if not a lot to get it better known with an increase in the number of visitors, and hopefully a good amount of return visitors as well. In addition to paying to advertise your website be sure to remember the essentials of making sure your website address is seen everywhere possible, such as on your business cards, maybe a bumper sticker on your car or on the cars of others, all your outgoing email messages and replies, and every other place you can imagine to put it, so people will see it, remember it and go to it.

Advertising With Google, Yahoo & FaceBook

Anyone can advertise with any of these online giants. You don't have to be a big company to advertise with them, but when doing any advertising anywhere you want to be sure to think your ad campaign through very carefully. It would be easy for an inexperienced person to incorrectly assume that if their book is being advertised on one or more of the world's most popular web sites, that their book is now on its way to the best-seller list. But this is not necessarily true. In their incorrect assumption the inexperieced person may make statements containing such positive phrases as, "it's a given," showing that the person is convinced the ad will do well.

Do your "pre-ad research" very well in order to get the most bang for your buck. Make sure you put your ad or ads in a place where not just the most people will see them, but the most appropriate people as well.

I have advertised books online using companies such as Yahoo, Google and FaceBook and although expensive I found all of them to be pretty effective as far as getting a good amount of clicks that bring visitors to my website, but as far as resulting sales are concerned I cannot recommend this type of advertising. It's fine if you have a very unusually good book, already well known that is selling like crazy and you know pretty much for sure that visitors to your site from the giant sites are coming over specifically to buy your book.

If your advertising does not include your website as a destination, but rather directs people right to the bookstore, online or off, it will be a little more difficult and will take more time to find out what the results are, if the bookstores do not have visitor and sales statistics immediately available. An effective ad campaign could be something that sends the prospective buyers to Google Book Search, where they can preview parts of your book, then select which online bookstore from which they want to buy your book.

Google Book Search has statistics immediately available for your use. As for the number of sales that result from the linked bookstores, this may not be immediately available, but the visitor stats from Google Book Search can give you a pretty good inidication of how well your book is doing in sales as well.

There is nothing in the least wrong with advertizing your books on these giant sites as an introductory type of advertising. Although I have managed to create ads where I paid an average of $.18 per click, the cost for each person going to your website and seeing your book could range from around $.75 to $1.00 or more. It is very suggestible to first run a test ad and carefully examine the results before committing a lot of your advertising budget to a major ad campaign.

You will find that you do much better by narrowing your target market. If your budget will permit you may want check into advertizing with the online bookstores such as Barnes an Noble, or at least in a book section of the search engine, which many of them have. Depending upon many factors, including the popularity of your book, it would only serve logic that your ROI would be better with the online bookstores and other appropriate sites than with the search engines and social networking sites.

Again, it can be easy to think incorrectly that advertising in the most "generally" popular places will result in book sales. A website with enormous amounts of traffic, but not specifically narrowed to your target market may likely not be at all a strong method to use in selling your books. With all the other ads being displayed the millions of visitors may never see your ad. If you are fortunate enough to have a runaway best seller on your hands you can probably do well advertising almost anywhere, but you will still increase your sales by placing your ads in the most appropriate places.

FaceBook, Google and Yahoo all have good advertising programs available. My experience with all of them found me favoring FaceBook. FaceBook has an easy to use Ad Manager and their rates seemed much better than Google or Yahoo. It cannot be mentioned too much - providing you have a healthy budget for advertising your books online or otherwise, it would be a very good idea to thoroughly do your research before spending your money.

With just about any company you place an ad with you will find statistics and/or demographics of at least some kind, for example how many males in any given geographical area verses female are book readers, and quite a number of other useful statistics that may be helpful to you in making your decision to run an ad or not. Do not place an ad without looking at the statistics. If you do you could easily be throwing your money away. And if you are able to do so it's also good to not just blindly accept that the stats are true, you can also confirm those statistics. For example if you have your website with a hosting service that provides statistics you can also use Google Analytics and see how the two match up. I have done this and found for the most part the comparison to not be perfect but fairly close. No one needs to be terribly concerned by small discrepancies but you will know something is way off and needs to be looked at closer if you notice something that completely does not make sense. For example, you are getting sales but do not see a large number of visitors. You know something is not quite right. Or the reverse, there is an enormous number of visitors but no resulting sales.

Free Advertising

In addition to social networking as mentioned in Chapter Seven, if we look around it's easy to find pretty good of sources of free advertising. You may remember things like the neighborhood Nickel Want Ads where people list all kinds of things they want to sell. Now days some of these small want ad papers are national and are on the web as well.

An example of some free advertising is Craigs List with many categories and listings in all major cities in the U.S. It's easy and free to post your listings with photos and links to your website. You can post as many ads as you want at no charge. The only cost is a little of your time each week to place free ads. When I first looked at Craigs List I didn't think much of it, but after placing a few free ads the results were surprising. It certainly won't make you rich but you will get some results from your listings in the books section.

Marketing Tools
FaceBook

With hundreds of millions of users, about 350,000,000 worldwide in December 2009 and over 100,000,000 of the users in the U.S., FaceBook is the largest of the social networking sites connecting people and companies together all over the world. FaceBook started in the 1990ies and was at first used mostly by college students, and has grown since 2004 to become the largest social networking site. In chapter seven ideas are given about how to best utilize the many features of FaceBook and other social networking websites to help market and sell your books.

weRead

Owned by LuLu Publishing weRead.com has a very attractive and useful application on FaceBook. If your book is published by LuLu it automatically goes into the weRead database. When a FaceBook user activates the weRead application, it makes posts on the user's profiles and shows on the home page of other users what books the users have read, with links for others to also select the book, preview and purchase it.

The weRead program has a feature called Chuck a Book that very nicely allows the users to suggest books to friends. The Chuck a Book feature does have a limit. It will allow you to send the book invite to all your friends but only 20 friends per book at a time and a limit of about 60 friends per day. Although the Chuck A Book utility is a very nice feature, as with any of the many social networking features you want to use it sparingly and not chuck too many books at your friends too often or you will find the number of friends on your friend list declining. One Chuck per book for each of your friends would be a wise amount, since your books are also listed on your weRead bookshelf that is on your profile, which your friends are able to see if they have a further interest after you have Chucked your book at them.

Be sure to create tags and keywords for your books on the profile for your book on weRead in order to make it easier for visitors to find your book when they are doing searches.

Twitter

Twitter is likely the second most popular of the social networking websites and is rapidly growing in popularity. I cannot say that it does or does not have all the features that are available with FaceBook, since I have not used it nearly as much as FaceBook, but it is another very popular form of socializing for many people and getting to know new people who may be interested in your books. The Twitter website looks to be ideal for someone building a list of fans and wants to keep the fans up to date with the latest information. Like FaceBook, Twitter is free to join and there is no cost to use it.

YouTube

YouTube is an excellent way to cleverly promote your book with videos. Particularly if you would like to create a humorous video and it gets popular this can result in a large number of visitors to your website or wherever you have your book listed. YouTube is a free service with a lot of features where you can post your videos. It also has paid advertising available.

I've used YouTube extensively with very good results at no cost for advertising airplane movies that I have produced. If you post a video that goes viral, a term meaning that your video is spreading in popularity like a virus, YouTube will invite you to sign up for a revenue sharing program they have available in conjunction with Google's Adsense program. With the revenue sharing program there will be content specific paid for ads placed next to your video, and when someone clicks on the ad you get to share in the proceeds of the advertising money.

SitePal – Talking Characters

If you have a website of your own or decide to create one in addition to all the other marketing tools that exist, you may want to consider using talking characters to add some life to the descriptions to your books. A picture is worth a thousand words and it would seem that a talking character could be a plus of some kind. At least it seems like that to me since I have used talking characters on my websites for a number of years now, and have found them to be an enhancement to other content that I use. SitePal has a very comprehensive free tutorial you can try in order to get an idea of how good the service is before you sign up, as well as a free two-week trial period.

The only source of talking characters I am aware of is SitePal at www.sitepal.com, a subsidiary of Oddcast. They have packages that range from $120.00 per year and up. I use a package that costs about $200.00 per year and gets the job done quite nicely.

For a few hundred per year you can select from a large variety of talking characters or create your own by uploading photos, and accompany the characters with different text-to-speech voices, make your own voice recordings and upload them, or use voiceovers of professional voice actors that do cost more but may be worth the difference in the quality of sound and professionalism.

A feature called Photo Face is available where you can use a photograph of yourself or someone else and convert it to a speaking character. I have used Photo Face and found that it worked quite well as long as you use a photo where the subject is close enough to the camera when the shot was taken, and in an upright position, without the head tilted too much one way or the other.

There are many readymade backgrounds to choose from with a number of categories such as business, holidays etc., or you can upload your own custom backgrounds from your own photos. Not all the available text-to-speech voices sound good. Some sound artificial and don't work out at all for me, but of the ones available I manage to get a few that I like to work very well, and it's easy to record your own voice scripts and upload them. If you don't want to deal with software to record your own voice scripts you can record the voice scripts by telephone with a toll-free number provided.

The tech support at SitePal is via email and is pretty good. I have used it a number of times with acceptable responsive turnaround that got the problems resolved in a timely manner. As with most applications on the Internet SitePal works best if you keep your own equipment well maintained and up to date. If you use an old computer and old software, such as an older version of you web browser you may have problems, like slow page loading and so forth that will probably improve if you upgrade your computer and web browser. At the same time it can be helpful to also have older equipment and older software on a second machine to also see how things look to people who have not yet upgraded their hardware and software. If someone complains about content that is on your website your first question to them should be what hardware and software are they using.

Zazzle – POD Advertising Items

Zazzle at www.zazzle.com is an excellent and very useful company that uses a print on demand system where you can advertise your books or anything else on printable items such as t-shirts, coffee mugs, mouse pads and calendars. Zazzle pays you a percentage of what is sold. They have available a very attractive automatic scrolling display that is done in Macromedia Flash, which you can put on your website for visitors to see. The code for the scrolling display can be embedded in as many pages of your website as you like. With Zazzle you can create t-shirts and other print on demand advertising items with your custom images and messages that you can give away at parties, book signing events and so forth.

When you create a free account with Zazzle you have your own storefront page, and the scrolling Flash banner advertises the items that are in your storefront. Visitors to your website may click on any of the items that are scrolling on the Flash display, which takes them to your storefront on the Zazzle website where they can purchase the items with your advertising message on it. You can see an example of how I use the Zazzle scrolling banner on my website at www.momentsofmagicphoto.com. You can signup for free with Zazzle to create your own advertising items. With Zazzle there is no charge to create as many advertising items as you want, which are all displayed for sale in your Zazzle store. All the advertising items are made-to-order or printed when ordered.

Slideshows & Music Videos From Slide.com

I accidentally and pleasantly discovered Slide.com when making a new friend on a social networking site and was happy about the find. I looked at the website my new friend had posted which was a site for the company she worked for, and I saw a very attractive slideshow that was displaying pictures of her place of employment.

Slide at www.slide.com is advertising supported, does not cost anything to join, and they have music videos as well as slideshows, with a large selection of good quality music from various artists. The music plays along with your photos that you select for your slideshow or music video. You create a slideshow or music video at no cost simply by uploading your own photos, arranging the order of your photos, selecting the music and format you want to use. The music, format and photos being used in your slideshow or music video can easily be changed at anytime on your website from the Slide website, without re-imbedding the code into your website. You can see a sample of how I use the Slide music video on my website at www.momentsofmagicphoto.com with photos of some of my book covers being used in the slideshow.

The music selections are licensed by the artists, many of which are newer artists who are making their music available in order to get it better known.

Research Tools

Doing good research is a very essential step in the process of publishing and selling your books. For a fiction or non-fiction book you need to search the Internet before deciding upon the title or author's name, verify and confirm information for your non-fiction book, and check the traffic ratings of companies that you intend to spend advertising dollars with, and a good many other things. It's all at our fingertips and easy for us to use and sad for us if we don't, when we find out after our book is published that we really should have done our homework.

Alexa.com

It always pays to do our homework. It's easy to look and see how much traffic an online company has before advertising with them. You can check any of the top 100 online company's traffic rankings with Alexa.com. This website provides many statistics about the largest companies on the Internet, as well as how long they have been in business, number of employees etc. Getting the facts on a company is certainly something to have on your checklist and should be done before spending advertising dollars. If they are not on the top 100 list it does not mean they are a bad company, it just means you don't have access to their traffic and other statistics.

With Alexa you will find that you can not only view the Internet traffic stats of a particular company, you can also check the company's reputation and compare a company's stats with the stats of a number of other companies. For example, you can look up the traffic ranking for Google, then type in Yahoo.com and FaceBook.com for comparison purposes and be able to see which company is number one, two and three, in traffic, user sessions and other statistics. This kind of comparison can be done with any company on the Internet that is in the top 100 companies regarding traffic ratings. Companies that are not in the 100 top companies list will not show up.

Wikipedia

If you have used the Internet to any extent and searched for just about anything you have undoubtedly read about things on Wikipedia. It almost goes without saying that Wikipedia is a very good source of data. The name comes up on almost any search we do. As a not for profit free online encyclopedia Wikipedia at www.wikipedia.org is supported by contributions from its users, and is an outstanding resource for researching almost any subject that has reached a reasonable level of popularity. It can be used to research famous people, companies, countries and just about any popular subject you can imagine. You will notice that when you do a Google search on just about any popular subject, a link to Wikipedia will show at the beginning or very near the beginning of the search results. Wikipedia is one of the most popular sites around and has very high traffic ratings.

Google & Google Book Search

It would be nearly impossible to log onto the Internet and not see the name Google and eventually find yourself on the Google site. This is because it is the most visited site on the web with a vast number of features, including being an excellent source for researching everything. Nearly everyone in the world who uses the Internet uses Google and often on a daily basis.

In addition to being an excellent resource for doing searches, Google has a book search feature where you can list your books using the book preview feature, and includes links to where your books can be purchased. The book search program also makes reports available to the authors for how many times each day visitors have viewed the books, how many pages of your book have been previewed, and how many visitors clicked on the link that takes them to the bookstore where your book can be purchased.

Keep in mind that like most of the advantages and desirable features available on the web than can help sell your books, Google Book Search is not an automatic thing when your book is published. The book search is something you have to sign up for in order for your books to show up on the Google Book Search. It is a relatively simple process, but you do have to do it. You have to first create an account with Google, add the book search partner program to your account and upload the content for your books.

And it is good to know that as of early 2010 Google has added to it's book search the feature of allowing authors to make their books available via electronic download, similar to Amazon's Wireless Whispernet for its Kindle Book Reader.

CHAPTER SIX

Learning From The Mistakes Of Others

For many of us, particularly those who tend to turn the channel when all that unpleasant news comes on, it seems that we need to be reminded every now and then about how things are in the financial world in which we live. It's easy for some of us to be naïve and unsuspecting souls, that seems to create opportunities for the unscrupulous to take advantage of us. The shysters operate on the principal that there are many unsuspecting people around, standing there with all that money in their hands, so why not take advantage of them?

Every few years or so it seems that we see a streak of white-collar crime happen, and that's only what we find out about. That's pretty much what happened in 1929 with the stock market crash, a few people play a confidence game on the masses, get everyone into the over-confident buying frenzy, and then the confidence guys pull the carpet out from under everybody when nobody seems to be looking. And what happened in 1929 continues to happen again every few years even if on a smaller scale, the savings and loan scandle in the 1980ies, the dot.com scandles of the 1990ies and the Ponzi schemes of the 2000s. And of course we know it will happen again, and many of the honest people never seem to learn the lesson, that if it seems too good to be true it probably is not true, and is probably something to stay away from.

But even with the problems of white-collar crime that goes on all the time, that only gets exposed from time to time, almost in a cyclical patern, it's certainly not the case that the entire world has gone to hell in a hand-basket regarding finding reliable and ethical people and firms with which to deal. There are still a lot of very good people and companies, but because of the crimes of a few there can easily exist generally a low level of confidence, which is why we just have to work all the harder to accomplish what we want and get things done right.

Beware Of Sleazy Offers

It's important to remember what not to do, just as it is to remember what you should do. If you submit a copyright registration to the Library of Congress, which is a good thing to do, you may soon find that your name and address is now on a mailing list, or a number of mailing lists, and you will start to get a number of seemingly attractive offers in the mail from publishers and agents of all kinds, making promises to you that they will in no way keep. Some of them can be legitimate offers but many will be junkmail that should be thrown away. You will have to make your own decision on that based upon the material you get from them and research you do before deciding.

We can't blame the Library of Congress. Everything registered there is a matter of public record. It's the same when you apply for a business license from the city in which you reside. It's public records and everyone and their dogs, whether they are good or bad dogs, now have access to your name and address and phone number. That is something many of us may find a little scary to think about but it is very true, and something that will be discussed further in Chapter Nine, namely the matter of business and personal security.

Junk Mail From Phony Agents & Publishers

It can sound very tempting. If you even read the junk mail you might find yourself being tempted to respond to one of the very legitimate looking offers, complete with the phony success stories and all, which will lead you down the primrose path to the poorhouse. Even if you have money to burn your time has to be worth something. There are many charlatans around that are waiting to take advantage of unsuspecting new authors by taking their money and promising them the moon. Your money will be wasted on everything from reading fees to large sums for the printing of books that no one will ever get a chance to read. It would seem that people selling these kinds of so called services depend a great deal on what we do not know, which is why it's important for us to learn as much as we can about the best mehods versus the worst methods.

At the same time there are very talented people who can review your manuscript for you and perform other services as well, for a fee that might be well worth the cost, particularly if you are quite new to writing. In the days before the Internet several of my books were reviewed by agents, some of them of which were very successful for many years and to whom I paid fees of a few hundred dollars, and found the reviews to be well worth it in the learning process. During the same period I also had books reviewed by agents at no cost, where the review and advice was valuable to me. This is still possible today if someone is new and would like to get some good professional reviews of their work, which can help them a great deal, but the new person should research and select the agent well.

Do Good Agents or Publishers Ask For Money?

Some of them will ask you for money, and that's perfectly okay if you get something for you money, hopefully a great deal of something. If you are going the conventional publishing route and your book is something that an agent or publisher see as a potential asset to them, they will never ask you for money. If your book is good enough the most you will pay is the cost of the paper to print your manuscript, and the postage to put it in the mail.

If you're going the self publishing route you know you will have to spend something, but it shouldn't be much and doesn't have to be much. It's better to be with an agent or publisher that can help you with self-publishing or co-publishing and develop your own marketing plan if you do not have the money to hire a good public relations or advertising firm to do the job for you. POD publishers will try to get you to buy a lot of copies of your books, but that's normal. They make money from that and they should. That's part of their business.

If you have a promotional event of some kind you may want a bunch of copies of your book to sell, give away as prizes, or include in a package of some kind, a charity event for example where people get a signed copy of your book for donating to the charity your are sponsoring etc. And of course you get your own books wholesale.

When you have a publisher that helps you with the self-publishing, gets your book into nice looking print, makes it available for electronic distribution, and assists you a lot in getting it into all the bookstores, don't sarcastically blame the publisher if your book still isn't selling. Instead realize that the publisher can be a big help to you with marketing, but the bulk of the marketing may likely be up to you or your advertising agency.

Don't Spend The Royalties Just Yet

Do yourself a favor and make sure the royalties or the money from your book commissions is in your bank before you spend it. It's all too easy to make the mistake of thinking that because your book is now in print and on the all-powerful Internet that you just struck it rich, and can go about the happy and carefree activity of buying all your friends a house. Instead check your mailbox or bank account to see if the royalty commissions have been deposited to your account, and if not look at the visitor statistics of your website and other sites where your book is listed and see how many people have been visiting and seeing your book.

If it happens for some strange reason that the money is not in your mailbox or did not get deposited to your bank account, then do some kind of advertising in order to get more people to visit your website and the bookstores. And do not think that because your book is now listed on Amazon or other big booksellers that you are home free. Instead look at the traffic ranking for whatever site your book is on. You can look up the traffic rankings on Alexa.com and get comparison reports for the sites where your book is listed. And if it doesn't look good go somewhere else or maybe find a number of other places for your book that have more traffic, with a better tarketed market that will hopefully be more effective.

Don't Assume Anything

Not to grind this idea to death or make you feel you are totally alone in the battle, but getting your books published and sold is a matter of continually staying on top of the big picture and making sure things get done. And the one who has to stay on top is you, because no one is going to do it for you, no matter how good those rumors sound that you may have been hearing. The following is an example of where making assumptions can lead to disappointment.

On my web site I have a few calendars that I published along with my books. I was excited when getting an email message from the publisher, informing me that some of my calendars were being selected for listings on Amazon, which would be happening in a few days. The publisher is the one who makes the decision regarding your material being good enough to be distributed somewhere, and lets you know where and when it will be distributed. But you are the one that has to verify and confirm that it does get distributed and distributed correctly.

The calendars I have displayed on my website may be viewed with a very attractive preview technique that shows the photos and months of the year to visitors before they make their purchase. Any normal person would "presume" that what was going to be displayed on Amazon would be something attractive as well, maybe something similar to what I have displayed on my website. But "presuming" things can result in leaving a sour taste in one's mouth.

When I looked on Amazon I was shocked and nearly died laughing when seeing that yes, my calendars were listed but with absolutely no photos at all. They only had text listings with a note mentioning "no photos available." Maybe it's a new concept I missed out on somewhere, a new idea to leave a little more to the reader's imagination. Can you imagine a calendar with no photos, or someone actually buying a calendar without any photos on it?

Fortunately I was able to immediately upload some photos for the calendars onto Amazon, but it would have been really nice if the publisher had included some photos with the calendars, or at least mentioned to me that they would not be putting photos on Amazon along with my calendars, but there had not been anything about it mentioned. The publisher had obviously did a sloppy job of listing my calendars on Amazon, without having anyone checking or confirming in the least that it had been done properly with accompanying photos.

Even with all the wonderful technology at our fingertips, and all the wonderful people helping us, to successfully publish and sell our books it's almost as if we have to pretend that we are a secret agent of some kind on a very dangerous mission filled with booby traps and pitfalls everywhere we turn, who can trust no one and must verify and confirm all data with our own eyes, in order to survive in this world. Maybe this is why it's referred to as self-publishing? When involved with any kind of publishing we find that it's necessary for us to remember and stay on top or things lest the publishing becomes suicidal publishing.

Don't Hobbyhorse Your Friends

It's fine to mention to your friends and family that you have a book out and maybe give some of them an autographed copy or at least a business card so they will know where they can buy your book, but do not completely rely on your friends or family for your book sales. If you do you might find that you soon have fewer friends, unless your friends and family are the kind that want to throw a book-signing party for you, but don't count on it. Be sure to find other people to talk to about your book and use marketing methods that will attract more eyes, especially if your friends and family don't get around to the book-signing party for you, and are instead found running and hiding as fast as they can.

Make it known to them that your books are there and ready to be previewed and bought, but be subtle about it and let them think it was there idea to buy your book. Rely mostly on other marketing methods for your book, and in time your friends will see how well you are doing with it and feel left out if they don't buy a copy and have you sign it for them. Most your friends will gladly accept a signed copy of your book if you give them one, but the objective is to get most of them to buy it. Other than maybe a few of your closest and best friends do not give your books away.

Don't Expect To Be Pampered

By now you should know better than to assume anything. But if you don't know better and really do have a habit of believing everything you hear and trusting everybody, it's time to change your way of thinking, and time to change your habits, by not assuming anything. Develop a habit of looking before you leap and knowing before you go. Do not make the fatal mistake of assuming that now that you are with a publisher they are going to do everything for you, because they most certainly are not. Do not erroneously assume that a publisher or some kindly old editor somewhere named Merlin is going to correct your typos, page formatting or anything else. There is only one person who is going to do that and we know who that person is.

The publisher has a big job to do and it does not include babysitting people who want or seem to think they need everything done for them. Publishers do their jobs and we have to do ours. When that book gets submitted to that publisher it better be right, because guess what? Chances are very good that they are going to publish it with all those typos and junk you left in it. If you are lucky a publisher may kick your book back to you if the margins are not correct in the manuscript you submit to them, but don't count on it. It's more likely the case that very few human eyes if any will see your manuscript before it gets printed into that paperback or hardcover book, or gets put into the electronic download format.

Do not be surprised to get a proof back of your book that you cannot read because that left margin is too small. In today's automated and electronic world you would be surprised at the number of things that slip through the cracks of the system unnoticed by the human eye. Particularly when doing self publishing what you submit is to a large degree being submitted to a computer system and unseen by the human eye. What you submit has to be letter perfect, no matter how many times you have to proof it, because absolutely no one is going to do it for you. Even in the best of economic times quality assurance is something that not all companies put up there as a real big priority.

Critics Are A Dime A Dozen

Unless you can see that the criticism is really constructive and valuable to you by adding some good innovative ideas, do not listen to critics, especially if they happen to be your friends or people holding themselves out to be your friends. Although it is true that constructive criticism can be a help to you in some cases, you will find often that critics are a dime a dozen with a low self-esteem, and the best way to compensate them is to cut a dime into twelve pieces and ask the critic which piece of the dime they would like.

If a friend reads your book and they give you what you can see is a fair evaluation then that is different, and the person is maybe really a good friend. But many times you will find that your friends do not know what they are talking about on most subjects, let alone the subject of writing books. When taking advice from a friend ask yourself this. How many books has your friend written, published and sold? Do your research well. Use your own judgement and make your own decisions, and let the insecure critics find somebody else to talk to. It's good to Look and Don't Listen. But if you want to talk to people talk to those who have been down the road and know what they are doing and what they are talking about.

Proof Your Ads Well Before Approval

If you are doing some advertising for your book be sure to proof your ad several times before clicking the go button. Review not only your ad copy but the entire ad campaign idea and sequence. Make sure to think the entire process through very carefully.

For example, let's say you are going to run an ad for your book that is available in both paperback and download, the paperback version being about $30 and the download version for about $5. If you think it through very carefully you will put the link in your ad to the download version since it's only $5, and you realize quite well that your paperback version is way overpriced, a mistake that you are not at this point able to correct. So, you get in a hurry and approve your ad to run with the ad linked to the paperback version of your book, and the result will at best be a good number of clicks to the paperback but no sales whatsoever. Let the potential book buyers see the $5 price for the download version first. They will be able to select the higher priced paperback version if they prefer.

The download versions are gaining in popularity but are not yet as popular as the paperback or hardcover (downloads about 35% of the market), but on the sales page for the downloadable version there is also a link to the paperback version. It's the simple psychology of first displaying to the buyer a lower price rather than the higher price. In many instances the author makes as much on the downloadable version as they do on the paperback.

The Pricing Of Your Book

During the writing and publishing of our book we will probably be researching quite a number of things, such as "is there a book out there that already has the title I want to use," or "is my name the same as sixteen gazillion other authors?" The comparative prices of books that are in the bookstores is another item we want to look into before we click the final go button for publishing our book. Research the prices of books in the bookstores, online and off, and prior to publication keep an eye on what the price of your book is going to be, for paperback, hardcover, other sizes and download. If possible make sure the price of your book will be competitive with similar books that have been published, so that the price of your book is not even a consideration to the potential buyer.

You don't want your book to be overpriced. Maybe your book is good enough or so good and in demand that people will pay for it whatever the price, but then again maybe not. You do have control over the price of your book. The price and cost of the printed version of your book will be more than the download version because of the cost of paper and shipping. You have control of both prior to publishing the book, but after publication you may not have control over the prices and costs without possible additonal expense to you, and interuptions of sales.

The bigger your book the more the cost. POD publishers have cost calculators you can use prior to publication, that will tell you exactly what the retail price will be, your royalty and your cost for getting copies for yourself. A paperback version is going to cost less than hardcover. Use the cost calculator to compare the price of your book for the different book sizes, paperback, 6x9, etc. Determine what the price of your book will be before publication to see how it compares in price to similar sized books that are in the bookstores. See what the difference in price is for your book in different sizes, hardcover, paperback, 6x9 etc. If the price looks too high you may be able to bring down the price by publishing it in paperback rather than hardcover.

If you publish a very large book it is simply going to be pricy in print, and many people do prefer print. They like things that are tangible, things they can hold in there hands, feel, smell and touch, which makes it very nice that tangible things have come into being such as Amazon's Kindle book reader and cell phones that books can be downloaded onto. Because of these kinds of devices the downloadable versions of books are becoming more popular. Downloadable versions comprise about 35% of the market as of fall of 2009 and are growing due to the growing number of the electronic book readers, which allow readers to wirelessly and almost instantly download books onto the devices, as well as PCs, MACs and a growing number of cell phones. The green thing is helping also, people wanting to help out by using less paper to save the environment.

Don't get discouraged or give up if everything doesn't get accomplished smoothly and without a lot of effort. Easy to say. You will get discouraged because it can get pretty rough, but keep on trying and you will find that with a lot of perseverance you will eventually succeed. It takes a lot of guts, patience and repetition to keep going in the face of adversity, and you will find if you use those things you will eventually come out on top of the situation and get that for which you have been striving.

CHAPTER SEVEN

Get All The Free Stuff You Can

Social Networking

In addition to the marketing methods mentioned in Chapter Five that are for the most part free, we would not want to leave out the subject of social networking. Particularly if your book has turned out to be popular, has started to sell or is selling very well, and if you have your computer or cell phone in front of you, and are logged in to one of the social networking websites, what you have sitting in front of you is nothing short of a potential gold mine.

On the otherhand if your book has just been published and is completely unknown the social networkng environments are places that can help you in getting it known. You do not want to hobbyhorse on your friends and family, and it may not be the biggest gold mine you will find, but you may as well get the gold that's in it while you are in the neighborhood. And you will find that social networking encompasses far more than just your friends and family. It's a big neighborhood. It is in no way an all inclusive marketing method, and not something we should rely on exclusively for selling our books or anything else, but to overlook it and not use it could be an oversight.

If you haven't heard the term social networking you probably haven't watched the news on TV or been on the Internet lately. It's quite the buzz and looks like it has a very good future. Social networking is a form of supplemental advertising for your book and the price is right. Other than the time you put into it, it's free. Among the most powerful of the bunch is FaceBook, which has hundreds of millions of users worldwide, 350,000,000 users as of fall of 2009. That's three hundred fifty million, in case you didn't count all the zeros, with about 100,000,000 of them in the U.S.

There is no cost to join or use it. FaceBook is about a hundred million dollar a year company that gets its revenue from advertising. It started in the 1990ies as a networking site mostly for college people and has grown dramatically since then. Although most its users are in the younger age groups there are people of all ages that use it for business as well as personal reasons.

You may not want to expect the world from it because people who use social networking do have a choice as to whether or not they want to see the things you post, but it has potential for adding to your book sales. And you will quickly find that many people who use it are there to sell something, just like you. For people who are relatively well known it's a great way to almost immediately add people to their list of friends and fan club. For people who are not quite as well known it can take some time but is quite possible to build a large list of friends easily numbering in the hundreds or thousands.

If you use a Penname or psudonym you may use it as your name when signing up for the social networking sites, so people will be able to find you and your books. You will notice that FaceBook allows both, your real name and a Penname as well which is a thorough method of making sure you get as much exposure as possible.

One of the things that makes the social networks so successful is that they have strict rules regarding pornography, racism, violence and subjects and activities that could be offensive to their users. The social networks enforce those rules by first giving warnings then deleting the account of the offenders. This is a beneficial thing for the users which provides a comfortable and pleasant environment in which they can socialize and share things with their friends. We also see a lot of very smart partnerships happening on the web with many of the biggest companies working together to make it all happen in one big cohesive environment.

Making New Friends

There are a number of social networking sites, Twitter being probably second in popularity. FaceBook has the most users and has the highest traffic ranking, and nothing is stopping anyone from using more than one social network. One can keep you plenty busy in your spare time. Many people who use FaceBook are under the impression that to request that someone be added to your friends list, you need to have previously known that person as a friend, co-worker, neighbor etc. That is generally the impression you can easily get, and the impression that FaceBook does tend to exemplify, but there is nothing wrong with making new friends, nothing stopping us from making friends with people we have never known, in other words complete strangers.

I demonstrated this to myself with an experiment by making many requests to complete strangers to become friends, and I went from about 30 friends to over 300 friends in only a few weeks. And you may very well be surprised to find that some of your new friends are very successful people and some with a great deal of influence that may be able to help you. I found quite by coincidence that some new friends that I added that I had not known previously, were in fact very successful entertainers. One was even an Emmy Award winning actor. You just never know whom you might meet in the social networks. It seems that everyone is there.

The best you could ever hope for to come from your use of the social networking, other than individuals buying your book, is making that connection with someone who is very well known, maybe even famous, someone who commands a lot of influence, who is someone that might possibly give an endorsement to your book. If you get that endorsement, of course it could result in many sales of your book. It doesn't get any better than that, and it in fact can and does happen.

There are people you may encounter who just made it in the entertainment business, the new face in town who just became known in a popular movie, and if you are fortunate enough to be added to their friends list you have done well, since they are new enough that their friends list isn't in thousands or tens or thousands or millions. This person could be good to know since they are completely elated with their success and now have so much influence, and like to help their friends and fans. With very famous people you will find many of them are very nice to know and are into helping others.

It may not seem likely that you will get added to the friends list of someone who has been famous for a while and has tens of thousands of friends. Even if they have someone adminster their friends list for them you are just another person trying to get to know them and are easily passed by, likely because no one is paying attention to your request to become friends. But it actually does happen and often since many people with celebrity status take a special interest in maintaining a large list of friends, as well as doing the same with a fan club, or have someone do it for them to keep the fans happy.

With the other people that are sell things on the social networks it may be possible for the two of you to do some mutual back scratching, you look at their items and they look at yours. You may encouner a number of new friends that are famous, who will tell you they will take a look at your book, and find that few of them if any ever do, but it only takes one who is famous to plug your book and get a lot of extra sales for you.

The way to get people you have never met to become friends is to make the request of them with a note explaining that no, you don't know them but thought you would take a chance and ask them to become friends. In my note I also explained to the complete strangers that I had gotten into the green thing, regarding my books being available for download which uses no paper, and also mentioned that if I did well I might just contribute to a few charities that might be some of their favorites.

People like charities. The subject and activity can be and is used in a business and/or personal manner as a method to help accomplish things, such as selling your books. I was recently invited by one of my social networking friends to a toys-for-tots fundrasing event where the tickets to the event started at $1,000 per person and went up to $50,000. The event was being held at someone's mansion, you know, the one that has the bunnies. When I noticed the prices of the tickets I thought to myself that they must be pretty nice toys, in more ways than one. The ticket for $1,000 admitted just one. For $5,000 I could take a few friends. The higher priced tickets included an ad in the company's magazine and so forth.

Use It Wisely

When doing my experiment of asking complete strangers to become friends, with an introductory note, I noticed that I got very few complaints from people to whom I made the Requests. People seem to like making new friends, and in the social networking climate as well as elsewhere, it seems that having a lot of friends is something of a status symbol. There may have been some of the complete strangers that ignored my request, and may have been annoyed or offended by the request, but if they were they didn't say. As it turned out I got more complaints from the social networking site itself than from those to whom I had made requests.

On several occasions I got an automated warning message from the FaceBook system, telling me that I was speeding and needed to slow down, since I might be doing something that could be annoying or offensive to other users. I'm not kidding about this in the least when I say that I got a Warning Speeding Ticket from FaceBook. Sounds silly, but it happened several times. I was making maybe 90 requests an hour, and okay, maybe that is going too fast. But I thought it was interesting that the FaceBook system neglected to let me know what the actual speed limit was for such an activity. The system probably should not have to tell me. Maybe I should just use better judgement. As a result I did slow down and only add a few friends here and there, and build up my list of friends on a more gradual basis in order to keep FaceBook's automated traffic cop happy.

The speeding tickets will happen since the social networking websites employ automated devices to detect hackers and spamers that could make things bad for the legitimate users. As a result if you are making too many friend requests or posts too fast you will get your warning tickets. And this is something we have to see as a good thing for all concerned. If you notice someone who makes posts continually, all day long, you will probably click that hide button next to the person's posts after getting tired of seeing so many of the same person's posts.

To provide an accurate picture of the use of the social networking thing, it would have to be said that it is useful mostly in getting your books known, and it's a gradual process that does not happen quickly. It's a system of making friends with people or connecting with people you already know, getting to know them or know them better, and "gracefully" letting them know you have a book there you would like them to take a look at, and doing it subtly enough so as to not offend them and make them lose interest in you as a friend. If your friends get the impression that the only reason you want to know them is to sell them a book, they may ignore you or even maybe delete you from the friends list.

It's wonderful if it happens but don't expect to make friends with people and have them buy your book right away. That probably will not happen. It is a process that takes weeks and sometimes months to develop, while you are also working on your other advertising and marketing processes, or writing your next book. It's something that can be a lot of fun, interesting and eventually hopefully profitable. At the very least you will have a number of new people who have become familiar with your book with a chance of their buying it because they know you. You must be very careful in approaching your friends about your book, so you don't turn them off and lose them as friends. If they decide they don't want to know you any longer it's only a matter of clicking that X on their friends list, and you go by-by.

Advantages Of Using Fan Or Business Pages

You can create a Fan or Business Page, as they are sometimes called, in addition to your personal profile. The fan pages are controlled from your profile account. If you try it you will see how it works. For example you can make a fan page for your book and invite all your friends to become fans of your book. Just like with requesting people to become friends, when you invite them to become fans most of them will join as a fan. There is a much higher percentage of success for the fan requests than the friend requests, because the ones you are requesting to become a fan are already friends. On the fan page there is a button that says, "Suggest To Friends," and you may use this with all the new friends you get.

You can get a lot more people to become fans by placing an ad. With FaceBook there is an Advertising link at the bottom of the home page and most other pages. The price can vary and go as high as $.75 or $1.00 or more per click, but I have added a few hundred fans to a page at an average cost as low as $.18 per click. With one of my fan pages for example I was able to bring the number of fans up to 350 for a cost of about $100. At $.18 per click that's 555 clicks with 350 of them also clicking the Become A Fan button, which is 63% ratio of people who click the ad that also become fans.

When any of your friends or anyone else becomes a fan, at their option, they will see on the home page updates or announcements that you make about your book from your fan page. When your friends first log in and see something you have posted from your fan page, they have the option to click the Hide Button, so they do not see it again, which they will most certainly do if you make a large number of posts or updates during a short period of time. They can also go to the Edit Options link at the bottom of the page, where they can un-hide your fan page so it will come into view again when they click on the home link at the top of the FaceBook entrance page.

There is an important and notable difference between a list of friends and a list of fans. People who are fans might not be on your friends list, but they can be invited to become friends, and friends can be invited to become fans. If you send a message to a friend a number appears on their message box at the top of their page, indicating they have an unread message or messages waiting, and displays the number of unread messages. The light does not go off until the friend opens the unread message. When you send a message to a group of fans from your fan or business page a number **does not appear** at the top of the page as it does when you send a single message to friends, but the fans do see the message when they look in their message box.

Although there may very well be a way to do it, generally you are not able to send a message to your entire list of friends, all at the same time, as you can with an email message, but you can easily do this with a list of fans. To send the same message to an entire list of fans it's called Update Fans which at one time was located on the upper left on the fan page. Last time I checked it was not there, but I did find it when clicking the Edit Page button near the photo for the fan page in the upper left corner of the page. It can change locations at any time and you may have to look around for it. You will notice that the social networking sites make changes to the site's structure, location of things and fuctions all the time.

The social network sites aparently set it up this way for reasons of not allowing people to annoy other uses by spaming or sending mass solicitations to their friends, which is actually a good thing. The administrator of a fan page can send the same message, or mass solicitation, to all the fans of the page at the same time, but the fans **do not** have their message light turn on to let them know they have a message, as it does when sending or receiving messages from friends. The message sent to the fans is there and the fans will see the message when they go into their message box. You have to use the Update Fans feature wisely and not too often, otherwise any of your fans can go down the left side of your fan page and find the link that says, "Remove From Fans."

See HubSpot in Chapter Five for additional information regarding fan or business pages.

On the front page of my website at www.momentsofmagicphoto.com it says, "Got FaceBook?" as well as other pages on my site. It also says, "Become a fan on FaceBook and win prizes!" I have a contest from time to time to attract visitors, like a free turkey, photo contest etc. When visitors to my website click on the FaceBook link they are taken to a fan page on FaceBook for Moments of Magic Photo. If they don't have a FaceBook account, they will be asked to create an account, which is easy to do with simply a user name, an email address and password. When visitors get to the fan page there is a button at the top they can click that says, "Become a Fan."

You can put whatever information you want on your fan page about your book or other things that you might like. Fans and other visitors to your fan page that are not fans may make comments, post links, photos etc to your fan page but only at your discretion, depending upon the permission settings that you as the administrator select. As the administrator you are allowed to select any of your fans to also be an administrator of your fan page. You have control over what visitors to your fan page are able to do with permission settings. The fan page will show a current list of your fans, comments by you and your fans and visitors, a list of links, photos etc., depending upon what you would like to allow to be displayed on your fan page.

As a user with a FaceBook profile, you can become a fan of other people's pages. Many of them are very interesting and some allow people to post links on their fan pages. Some of them allow you to post links to your website or your own fan page. I have used this with a significant amount of responses from people on the fan pages I have joined who have noticed my links or posts. I use electronic talking characters or models on my website that help make sales, and I have also posted links to the talking characters on people's or company's fan pages. The talking characters will say anything you program them to say, and there are a lot of characters and voices to choose from. See SitePal Talking Characters in Chapter Five.

Although repetition is important you must be careful to not look like a spamer by making too many posts in a short period of time, quite similar to the problem with making too many new friend requests too fast. Your social networking website will likely have an automated system that will tell you with a message that pops up, when you are going too fast or making too many posts on pages of which you are a fan, or when making too many requests for people to become your friends. Better to be conservative and just do a little each day rather than have your social networking account cancelled for what would be described as abuse.

Using a fan page or a number of them in conjunction with your social networking profile and your website must be done carefully and with good judgment. It's mostly a matter of using the system for a while in order to get a feel for it. I tend to engage in rather mature humor and have to be careful so I don't offend too many people. And on the subject of offending people we should say that this is something you don't want to do. You will never be able to keep everyone happy. At best you will only be able to keep most the people happy most the time. As your number of friends and contacts increase on your social networking account you will find it more and more necessary to pay attention to things you say and do.

Remember that what is free today may not be free tomorrow, and what is here today is sometimes if not often gone tomorrow, but fortunately if we see something is no longer around something else comes along to take its place that is often even better than what we had. Companies and what they offer are continually changing and we must constantly keep up with the changes to get the most benefit. At no time in history has there been such beneficial tools as what we now have at our disposal on the Internet. The social networking sites have done well in attracting and keeping users, but it is not at all downhill for them. They work continually to attract and keep as many users as possible, and make improvements all the time to their websites and features offered.

Event Planning

The social networking sites make event planning convenient and efficient. FaceBook has an event-planning feature that is easily to utilize for planning events and inviting your friends. It has an interface for you to send the invitations with a box for the friends to RSVP and keeps a record for you of how many have accepted, how many are thinking about it and so forth. This can be used to plan any kind of event you can imagine. For anyone who RSVPs to an event they get a reminder message by email and a reminder that displays on their home page a few days ahead of the event.

Toys For Tots & Other Charities

Any time of the year but particularly during the holidays you can combine your book-signing event with a charity of some kind. Send invitations to friends for a Toys-for-Tots or some other fund raising event that benefits a charity. The friends who attend the event pay for a ticket and get an autographed copy of your book. You can include the cost of your book in the cost of the tickets or work it out however you want.

weRead

weRead is owned by LuLu Publishing and has a very nice application in FaceBook that makes it easy to suggest your books to your friends. The suggestion feature is called Chuck a Book and allows you to select which of your friends to whom you would like to suggest your book. When you use the Chuck a Book feature it posts a note or notification to your selected friends about your book. weRead and your social networking site will help you keep to from sending too many suggestions by only allowing you to use the Chuck a Book feature a limited number of times for each of your books. It will allow you to send the book invite to all of your friends but only 20 friends per book at a time and about 60 friends per day.

Personal Matters

We all know that we should always present ourselves and our activities in as professional a manner as possible. Some of us get frustrated once in a while and at times really need to vent or blow off a little steam. And we don't always get along really with everyone else. The social networking environments are not the place to vent our frustrations or blow off steam, particularly if we are using it to help sell our books. We don't ever want to hang our laundry in public.

If somebody is having a bad day, is upset about something and needs to blow off some steam and get it out of their system, the following may be something that can help. If you do not know someone who is willing to listen to you vent in private and not repeat what you say, then write in a note exactly what you would like to say to the person or persons you are upset with in very exact detail, sparing no anger or hostilities. Then print out what you have written, read it again or maybe a few times, tear it up and delete the note. You will probably feel better after doing this and it will not negatively affect your social networking or chances of book sales.

It can also be the other way around. If you use the social networking like other situations in life where you relate with people, you may find it to be just the opposite, where you encounter someone who is very upset with you. It may be a situation where the person is somewhat mildly annoyed with you, maybe something you said or did, where you can resolve the situation with a simple apology.

Then again it may be someone who is a heckler and just wants to get under your skin or maybe worse in attempting to do some serious damage to your reputation by saying nasty things to you or about you. Although most people we encounter are of the nicer variety the hecklers do exist, if even just a few here and there, and we must be prepared to deal with them by ignoring them, if that works. If it doesn't work we can fight back and do damage to them if needed by deleting them as a friend or fan. If someone is a heckler you may disconnect the person from any and all association with you within the social networking site by using your permission settings.

We want to be careful in public by not saying or doing things to agitators or people we are angry with that other users are going to see or be expoed to. Most the people we encounter with social networking are very nice and pleasant, but it's good to keep in mind that there are crazy people in this world that want to raise havoc with the lives and objectives of others. In cases like this there does exist that delete button which can and maybe must be used in order to disassociate from the crazy person, and prevent them from doing harmful things. There is also a link to a reporting system where a report can be made about the crazy person, so that action can be taken by the social networking site.

In a year or so of using social networking I have had to remove about three people from my friends list. One was a person who was apparently a hacker who didn't seem to actually have an account with the network, and managed to use hacking skills to get in and make derogatory comments on my fan page. I reported the hacker and that resolved the problem. Another was a person who sent me a message with a link to a virus of some kind that I was fortunate enough not to allow onto my computer. I removed her immediately from the friends list. The third was a person who was supposedly a good friend for a while. Then this person became quite judgmental and very offensive and dominating as to how I should sell my books. She was making public comments of a negative nature that I thought were very inappropriate, with some self serving interest motivating the attacks. This person was also removed from the friends list. They were all removed without anyone else having to witness or be affected by the social turbulence.

We will find through experience that any of the social networking sites will not make or break our objectives for our book sales, but these networks and the features they offer can make a difference and help us if used properly.

CHAPTER EIGHT

Get The Attention

Getting people to stop and pay attention rather than continuing past the sight of our book is the objective we are seeking to achieve. There are many methods to catch their eyes or get their ears to perk up. We all have our own ways we like to do things. What works for one of us may not work for another but all of us have to do something that will get people to stop and take notice of what we have to offer and hopefully give it some serious thought. It could be a humorous bumper sticker, that dynamic book cover, a video on your website or an attention grabbing ad you place somewhere that will make the difference, but we know something has to be used to get and keep the attention long enough for the person to look at the book.

Ask For The Order

If getting your book into the bookstores has been done correctly you are effectively asking for people to buy your book. The bookstores are the major part of the plan, but you can bolster what you now have in place in the bookstores with some good press releases, listing on your website, social networking, ad campaigns and giving a business card to everyone you meet, all designed to get people to go to those bookstores and buy your book. We find that just putting our book somewhere for sale is not enough by itself to get the job done. Asking for the order is necessary and may involve many of these things that can help us in persuading the shopper or browser to go ahead and buy the books.

Use The Buy-Now Technique

The buzzwords of Buy Now seem to be where it's happening, or what makes it happen and have been for some time. Once you have gotten someone's attention through an ad or by whatever means, you then need to tell the person as well as ask the person to buy now. It's okay to ask them, but you must also tell them. Not buy tomorrow or next week, but Buy Now! Of course it's done in a pleasant way that can be described as a high level of demand, getting the shopper to act and make the purchase. It can be in the way of a humorous book cover or hilarious ad that impacts the shopper so effective, that we can say it absolutely demanded that the shopper buy the book.

It's the difference between what sales people refer to as soft sell and hard sell. Don't be afraid to offend people with the hard sell of buy now. It's not a matter of people thinking that you're not nice if you use hard sell. Remember that nice guys finish last, so don't worry about those that are going to change the channel when you tell them to buy now. Some will turn the channel when you tell them to buy now or when you ask them nicely. Can't get them all. You can get some sales with soft sell but you will get a lot more with hard sell. And we see hard sell everywhere we look. There's an ad on TV and you will notice that the ad says, "get your new car today!" It doesn't say, "Why don't you think seriously about getting that dream car you've always wanted?" There is a big difference between the two methods of getting the sale, as any sales professional can tell you.

And the sales professionals will also tell you that it often takes a good many times of telling the prospect to buy the product. I've heard sales people tell me that they closed the deal after as many as eighteen attempts, or eighteen times of asking and telling the prospect to buy the item. How many times do we see an ad on TV, just once? Not on your life! We see the same ad again and again and again until we are so sick of it that we are just about ready to go out and buy the product in order to shut the people up who are selling it to us, as if that were possible. It can and often does take a great deal of repetition for the idea to sink into the minds of the public.

Free Preview Method

It doesn't get any better than this. There's no limit whatsoever to how clever you can be in getting someone interested in your book. I have used a number of ads that describe some of the chapters of a book to give the sales prospects a limited preview of what's inside the book. If you have ever looked at books on Amazon, Google and many others you have probably noticed that with many of the books you can preview parts of the book before buying it. This is something that does require a little more work on your part or the part of someone who may be helping you market your book, and some authors don't like the idea of the preview and hope that the front and rear covers and description of the book will be enough to sell it.

Logic would tell us it's a good plus that would likley increase chances of sales. It's an available option well worth considering. Amzon also claims it helps make the books more searchable and easy to find. Why would so many bookstores and authors be using the preview or free-look, and ask authors who have not yet used it to consider using it with their books, if it was not something that resulted in some appreciable increases in sales? If it wasn't helping to create more sales they really would not be using it. When we buy a car or a number of many other large ticket items we can view it online and order it without seeing it in person, but most of us would rather see it, sit in it, smell, touch and feel it and drive it or try it before we buy it. The book preview technique is very similar.

Practice Makes Perfect

The difference between an amatuer golfer and a professional golfer would seem to be the amount of interest they have in the game, but it would also tend to have a great deal to do with the amount of practice or the number of games played. That would also seem to be true with many other activities. We've all heard the term "a natural," and some of us are truly born gifted, but most of us are not born with the abilities to do most things perfectly the first time. Once we've been through the game a few times it seems to become more comfortable, our interest level increases and we get better at it. This would also apply to publishing and marketing our books. That first time through can be almost painful, but when we have been down the road and back a few times it gets easier and we get better at it.

When publishing two books a few years ago it was done through a conventional publisher and I noticed with disappointment that the books never made it onto Amazon. Well, it did save me some work because I didn't have to worry about signing up for the free preview or Look Inside This Book feature. When I searched Amazon for the publisher the search only brought up book titles that were no longer in print. That was not at all an encouraging discovery, but having already signed the agreement with the publisher there was nothing I could do to improve the situation. It did teach me a lesson to do better research on publishers before selling my books to them.

Publishing two books in June of 2009 through LuLu Publishing proved to be a more rewarding experience. I noticed a message on my LuLu account page that said that my two books were Google Book Search Enabled. This was the first time I had been this route, having the books enabled for Google Book Search, and I incorrectly assumed that they would automatically show up on the Google Book Search. Silly me. So after a while I went into my account with Google and figured out how to add my two books to the Google Book Search program. The process was fairly easy and it seems to be a very nice program that allows readers to preview the books, before clicking on a link to the bookstores where they can buy them. It also displays to the author of the books how many people have previewed the books and how many have clicked on the bookstore links. Nice program, you just have to sign up for it and not think someone out there is doing everything for you.

A similar experience happened to me with Amazon. I'm on Google Book Search previwing my books, click on the link to Amazon and see they are for sale, but I notice on Amazon my books do not have the Look Inside This Book feature, and I tell myself, "well, Amazon is a pretty big bookstore, reportedly the world's biggest, they are obviously pretty busy and will get to it soon, I'm sure." Silly me again.

I guess when we are a little kid and have our parents do everything for us, we get so we like that kind of thing and tend to want to coast on it for a while. It's a nice life while we can get it but don't try to make a career of it.

When we have grown up and published a few books it's probably about time to realize that Mom and Dad and the tooth fairy have really high expectations of us and would really like for us at this point to go onto Amazon and sign up for the Look Inside This Book program, upload the content of your books, the front and back covers, and let Mom, Dad and the tooth fairy get a little rest.

So don't be too hard on yourself if you don't get it perfect the first time through. It can take some practice to reach perfection and some time as well.

CHAPTER NINE

Business & Personal Security - Scary But True

Security is not something any of us want to dwell on day and night, but we know we at least need to be aware of it and take some steps to protect ourselves. It would be nice if we could just go about the business of writing, publishing and marketing our books without having to be bothered by such things as security. But the subject of our safety seems to have come more to the forefront in recent times. For those of us who may want to cover the subject of security in more detail, I have another book coming out in the not too distant future that deals exclusively with the subject of business and personal security. In the following we will at least cover the basics.

What's all the paranoia about? What could security possibly have to do with our checklist for publishing and selling your books? Entirely a great deal. It can be a problem for us simply because we probably do not think like criminals. So, in order to protect ourselves from the criminals, maybe it's a good idea for us to take some time and learn how to think like criminals.

Identity Theft Or Worse

Not to be a complete pain by unnecessarily frightening anyone, but if you're identity has been stolen, or even worse, if you are not even around anymore you will not be able to publish or sell your books. We don't have to look far to notice what a dangerous world it is in which we live. We see increased security everywhere, which is something we have to do for ourselves as well on a personal and business level. This is particularly the case since so much of our work is done on the Internet where it's very important for us to keep things as secure as possible.

Internet security professionals will suggest that we change our passwords at least every 90 days, and use passwords that are difficult for the criminals to crack by using combinations of words, numbers and special characters such as the $ sign, % sign and so forth. They also suggest very good ideas such as do not in any way give your passwords to others, in person, by email, texting, or by accessing your financial accounts from your laptop computer when you are at that coffee shop with that very nice wireless but scary un-secure connection to the Internet. The professionals will also tell us to not write down our passwords, but to memorize them or use a password protection program that can be obtained or downloaded from various safe sources on the Internet.

You may recall hearing a friend or an older person mention a time when people didn't even bother to even lock their doors at night. It must have been nice but it's not that way now, and as an author you are in the public eye, you are out there in the market place selling your books, and need to pay attention to things having to do with security. It seems to us that most people are honest and not someone for us to be concerned with, but we also know that there are a few nasty people around that tend to make things bad for the rest of us in the way of stealing and things that even are worse.

Keep It Private

You may have noticed that many companies do not list their business street address, mailing address or in many cases a phone number on their websites. Keeping those things out of sight on the website is also for purposes of cutting down the amount of junk snail mail (regular mail, other than email) that a company gets, and the number of nuisance phone calls. But it can be for reasons of security as well. Unless your company is a walk-in kind of business there is no sense in advertising the location, particularly if most your business is done on the Internet.

If you register the domain name for your website the records associated with the domain name become a matter of public record, available to anyone in the world. Anyone using the Internet can easily lookup your domain name on a service known as Who Is, and see your name, business name, street, mailing address and phone number. I'm not at all comfortable with that and prefer to keep my company's information private. For a small additional fee each year the domain registration service will keep the information private.

You don't need a city business license to write and market your books unless you are also selling them directly to the public from your location. A city business license is a matter of public record also. I don't know if it's possible in most cities to request that information be kept private. I don't think it is in most cities, which is something I do not like, particularly if a person happens to have their business at the same location as their residence, which many people do.

Seeing how freiendly, sociable and pleasant most people are can give us a nice feeling. But it never fails to amaze me how so many people, almost in a childlike manner, will innocently open the doors of their homes to complete strangers. Far too many of us do the same with our electronic homes on the Internet. We see on the news all the time the frightening stories of home invasions, criminals knocking on people's doors disguised as someone from one of the utility companies, people getting robbed on the street by some guy with a badge and holding himself out to be a plainclothes policeman. Whether you have your business at home or not a good security camera system might be a very good idea, along with good locks of various kinds on the doors.

Email & Cell Phones Are Not Private

We all see the Spam each day, or unsolicited email that comes into our email inboxes, and all those ads that come with them, inviting us to buy this or that, invest in this or that, and hopefully we use a Spam filter and do not respond to any of those messages that ask us to accept a check but first send a check to someone in another country, along with your social security number just to make sure they have reached the right person. The reason we keep getting the Spam is because, believe it or not, there are people among us who actually respond to those offers.

Some of us may be under the erroneous impression that email is private. But unless we are using an encrypted email program it is not at all private, and most people do not use encrypted email. The same with cell phone conversations and texting. It's possible for email and cell phone communications to be intercepted by the prying eyes of criminals who have the equipment to do it. As to how many and how much criminals are eavesdropping on our conversations, there is no way of knowing. This is probably not something to be alarmed about in our everyday use of email and cell phones, but something we should keep in mind regarding the sending or receiving of very sensitive information that we want to absolutely keep private, such as credit card numbers, social security numbers etc. Unless there is a wiretap on a landline phone a fax sent over a landline is probably the most secure way to send sensitive information.

Social Networking Security

You will notice on the profile pages of people who use the social networking sites, most people list a minimum of personal information, most do not show a phone number, many show the email address, but no one ever lists their home residence address. The social networking companies have very good security systems with a good many privacy permission settings available for users that allow us to customize the security level of our personal profile. But it is up to us to use these privacy permission settings to our advantage. It is not done automatically by the social networking site.

It is worth taking a few minutes to become familiar with these permission settings in order to use them to increase our level of security. For example, suppose you want to list the name of the company you work for, your cell phone number, email and some things that you want available on your profile for your list of friends on that social network, but only to your friends and not everyone on the Internet. Well, let's check and make sure it is available only to your friends.

If we take a look at the permission settings on your account we notice that possibly everyone on the Inernet may not have access to your personal information, but they may as well have since everyone on the social networking site does have access to all your personal information, which numbers in the hundreds of millions of people. This is not at all what you want. So click a checkbox or two that makes your personal information visible to only people on your friends list. Even then, how safe is your personal information? Let's take a closer look.

A lot of the users of the social networks would likely tell us that they like the network because they can add only the people they want to their friends list. But let us keep in mind how easy it is for someone who is up to no good to somehow manage to get on our friends list. Remember what was mentioned in a previous chapter about how easy it is to get on the friends list of complete strangers simply by asking them to be your friend? As much as we may not want to think about it, the criminals are aware of that little trick also, and are probably even much more skillful at it than some of us.

A case in point is a conman who has been getting into the locker rooms of very famous sports teams, and making off with a lot of cash and jewelry to the tune of tens of thousands of dollars. He was seen on video surveilance cameras walking around a locker room of a visiting team, authoritatively with a clipboard in his hand and even wearing one of the team's sweatshirts. This is a very skilled criminal at work who has pulled off this crime in the Los Angeles area quite a number of times, and manages to not just smoothtalk his way past the hotel clerks, but also gets the hotel clerks to give him keys to the athletes rooms, simply by wearing one of the team's sweatshirts and telling the clerk he is with the team. This guy is so smooth and brazen that one witness mentioned seeing the conman hugging some of the members of the team, and yes, he was wearing one of their sweatshirts, you know, with the team's name on it and everything. What a charming guy.

And what kind of intelligence system does this very shrewd conman and thief use in his criminal activities? It turned out that among other things he was using the social networking sites to get his information as to where the visiting athletes would be staying. Where the visiting team will be playing is very much public information, but as to the hotel where they will be staying should be kept as private as possible, or at least we would think, not to mention access to the locker room and hotel rooms of the team.

A problem with many of us honest people is that we are too nice, trusting and don't ever think the way that the criminals think. We may not leave our doors unlocked at night but other than that many of us are sitting ducks when it comes to being easy prey for the smooth talking conmen that are looking for an easy mark.

CHAPTER TEN

The Right Stuff

If it happens that you have been applying ideas and methods you have found in this book, and maybe some of your own ideas and methods as well, and yet you feel like everyone is against you at this point, you find that no one supports you in your efforts, you get the silent treatment, people ignore you, criticize you and condemn you to others, then you are very likely on the right track and doing the right thing.

The ones who seem to be against you, ignore your requests for help, doubt you, criticize you and bad-mouth you to everyone else are extremely average people, who follow in the crowds of mediocrity and will never accomplish much beyond the realms of the dreary and very lackluster and useless status quo. Add to this the fact that they are probably severely upset by what you have been doing, mostly because of the fact that you are doing it and they are not, you are getting attention from it and they are not, then you again are dealing with some pretty average people.

The very same treatment has been given to people like the Wright Brothers, Edison, Lindbergh and so many others. Hopefully you are getting rave reviews from everyone instead criticism and the silent treatment. But if you are getting a lot of the silent treatment and the rest of the gloomy things, be sure by all means to continue doing what you have been doing, with even more determination to succeed.

Not everyone is capable of writing a book. And people who are critical of us, ignore us when we bring up the subject and/or give us the silent treatment have no reality on writing a book. The critics likely have no experience in the activity themselves, and it's not something that is at all real to them, and they are unable to accept the idea that you are writing a book. That's the simple mechanics of it.

Post Publishing

Unless we signed with that mamouth conventional publisher that has megabucks going into the marketing of our book, a big part of our checklist will deal with what we do after our book is published. Along with being excited and starting on our next book while the adrenaline is still pumping, there is probably a lot we need to do to keep an eye on with our book that just got released into the marketplace. A watchful eye on the sales reports and keeping in mind what we have done so far in our marketing processes, and what we have planned for the future will all be a part of it. A press release of some kind that will get things going, get the people searching the bookstores for our book, using our contacts or developing some to setup a booksigning event of some kind, and making sure there's enough steam behind it all so as to make sure we don't have a situation of too little too late.

It's like those guys in the circus we see flying from the cannons. There has to be enough powder in the chamber to insure the guy lands on the soft cushioned mat, rather than come in a few feet short of the target and land on the cold hard concrete. Anyone who has attempted to operate on a shoestring likely knows well of what is meant by too little too late. There were just not enough visitors to the website, resulting in even fewer visitors to the bookstores to get the book over the hump and onto the road to success. We want to make sure we are putting enough advertising power into our book marketing. And did we accept the help or good advice from friends or family, if they wanted to help, or did we go it alone and maybe ignore some good and useful ideas?

If it happens that we find that it looks like things in our marketing activities are at present too little too late, hopefully it's not too late to apply some of the things mentioned on our checklist that will make the difference and bring our book sales into an acceptable range, if not over the top and onto the best-seller list.

Although some of us may not realize it, having a book go viral and becoming a household name that tens of millions of people are clamoring to get their hands on, while at the same time staying completely annonymous with all that countless money going into our accounts would be a blessing and about as good as it could possibly get. You would get to reap all the wonderful rewards and benefits of your work without the adversities of being so well known that you cannot step outside the door of your house, without being mobbed by the hungry sensationalism grabbing photographers and press.

While there exists those of us who are still relatively unknown and have dreams of the idea of getting up on the stage, taking a bow with the spotlights on us and hearing the long and loud applause from the audience, others of us wisely know that this kind of glory ride is really not for us.

We recall reading or seeing a news report on the outcome of average people's lives who have won a lottery, and are surprised to see how badly it turned out for so many of them, how the sudden success with so much money was a shock to their lives so much that many ended up broke or deeply in debt not long after their big winnings. It perhaps makes us realize that there is nothing wrong with getting and having a lot of money and new responsibilities, but also hopefully makes us stop and think for a moment before we decide what to do with the money and the many aspects our lives that have changed so suddenly.

Media Impact, Politics & Public Relations

Before the Internet existed with all its so rapid communication features there was yet a world wide web that existed. There was a media, word traveled and had quite an impact but just not as fast and as effectively as it does now on the Internet. With all that speed and effectiveness now available at our fingertips it does us well to carefully consider what we want to put into the media, particularly about ourselves. We're careful to mention only the positive things and don't use the media for place to bare our souls in a confession like manner, or make a complete disclosure about our personal lives, because we know well that if we become really well known there are those in the media who will be doing plenty of digging into our backgrounds with plans of making it public.

Whether or not we chose to remain anonymous, if it is at all possible, or step onto the stage we learn or should learn that things are not at all the same as they used to be. It should be apparent to us that we have new responsibilities even if we remain as anonymous as possible. Careful thought is given to such things as do we want to abruptly stop knowing some of the people we have known but didn't really click with or like all that much, or maybe it would be better to keep them as friends and not create problems by leaving them in our dust.

Our new success could bring to mind memories of the changed lives of some who won the lottery with many of those lives not turning out at all good, some who so foolishly went on lavish spending sprees that left them broke or deeply in debt, and one even dead at the hand of a jealous former spouse. We also remember the best and most successful case being the couple who made few changes in their lives after winning the lottery, which seemed to kept them on the road to a quiet but normal life as possible.

Will The Media Work For Us Or Against Us?

An evident truth is that our income from just about any activity is proportional to how much and how well we relate with others. Making sure everyone feels appreciated is an important part of our relating with people, even with those who like to give us the silent treatment. Everybody likes attention and many will do some interesting and not always good things to get it if they feel they are not getting it.

When someone gets on the stage and accepts an Oscar they thank everyone from their landlady to God for everything in the world. We don't have to go that far after our book is published and in the marketplace and everyone is buying it. If our book is doing very well the first person we should probably thank is ourself. But whether they are buying or not it doesn't hurt anything and probably does more good than we realize to remember the little things in regards to how we deal with others that can make a big difference.

No one is going to be able to please everybody all the time. There will always be an agitator or heckler here or there. We just have to do the best we can by making sure we are considerate, don't ignore people, make nice comments about them whether it's true or not and keep smiling while doing it, sometimes even while we are being ignored or given the silent treatment.

We can see that there did exist a world wide web before the coming of the Internet. That was the world wide web of politics and public relations. It's still here and it still works, it just works better and faster now that it's on the Internet. It's wonderful, the idea of writing a fabulous book with an eye-catching title and cover, subject matter that people all over the world will readily search for and buy, and this does happen all the time. It's the supply and demand aspect of things. There is a big demand for something you have created, you put it out there, make it available to people who are looking for it. They come in droves and buy your book.

That is all very well and good but when we add what follows it could mean the difference in tens of millions of dollars in sales for our already very popular book. We see this happening all the time. Just watch any one of the popular talk shows. You will see very well known people of all kinds, and some that are becoming more well known on the talk shows, each and every one of them plugging their books, movies, music cd's and whatnot. Some of them may not in any way need more sales or more money but they do it because they can, they know how, they know the right people, or the right people call them because shows need people to make the guest appearances, and they go a head and do it. The business is there so why not take it? It's always the game of bigger and better that we know so well.

As to will we be satisfied with a somewhat above average number of sales and a very good amount of money that comes with it, and be content to quit while we are ahead, or will we be like the the others and keep going for more and more and more, the answer is yes, we will likely continue to keep going for more and more. Winning, success and the money that comes with it is a lot of fun and that's what it is all about. In fact it could nearly be impossible to stay out of the limelight if you are the author of that runaway bestseller. The talk shows would be hot on your trail because they need those guest appearances to keep their ratings up. Nice problem to have.

People who are well known politicians or have a place on the world's stage in any popular form get an automatic bonus of sorts in that they are almost assured of their book selling, if they write one or have one written for them, simply because of the fact that they are so well known. And this is so true that it would be difficult to believe that a well-known politician or anyone who is well known does not write a book, unless they really have no interest in the matter and really do not want to do so. Not that writing any book is ever a piece of cake, but if someone famous does write their book, it's simply an extra few million dollars for them at the minimum if they are at all well known to any degree. For those of us that write a book who are not well known it is a matter of using the tools mentioned in the preceeding chapters, that are at our fingertips to make that book very well known. Then when we become better known we can hopefully enjoy the benefits that famous authors have of the big advances from the large publisher, eager to publish our blockbuster, maybe even before we have completed the manuscript for the blockbuster.

It is hoped that in reading this book you have gained a lot of useful ideas, tips and methods that you have been or will be able to apply to the publishing and marketing of your books, and that these things are of a great deal of help to you, and will be for a long time to come.

Good luck and the best of wishes to you in your writing, publishing and marketing activities.

Rex Lee Reynolds

About The Author

Rex Lee Reynolds is an American engineer who has worked as a quality assurance engineer and web developer in the health care industry for the past fifteen years. He has been writing books since the mid 1980ies, has written a dozen or so fiction and non-fiction books, and has published five books to date including this book, two fiction and three non-fiction. He has a number of other non-fiction books in the planning that are a series of checklist self-help books. He has experience in dealing one-on-one with literary agents and publishers in the conventional publishing industry, with two books published by a conventional publisher. His experience in self-publishing has resulted in the publishing of three books to date, two fiction and one non-fiction.

The author is currently an engineer in the field of computer sciences, which began in 1995 with the development of WiseGuy InterActive Word Game for Kids and WiseGuy InterActive MathBox for Kids, still being sold through www.digitalriver.com. He is also experienced in the fields of real estate, insurance, finance, healthcare, aviation and entertainment.

Most recent books published in June of 2009 are Trouble in Sleepy Springs, suspense crime mystery and Closet Full of Teddy Bears, a number of romantic situation comedy stories. These two books are published by LuLu Publishing at www.lulu.com and are available at www.lulu.com and www.amazon.com.

He is a professional photographer, owns and manages two businesses, a modeling and talent agency at www.momentsofmagicphoto.com and an airplane enthusiast movie business at www.airshowmovies.net.

Index